THE
PERFECT
WIFE

The Life and Choices of Laura Bush

ANN GERHART

SIMON & SCHUSTER
New York London Toronto Sydney

 SIMON & SCHUSTER
Rockefeller Center
1230 Avenue of the Americas
New York, NY 10020

SIMON & SCHUSTER and colophon are registered trademarks
of Simon & Schuster, Inc.

For information regarding special discounts for bulk purchases,
please contact Simon & Schuster Special Sales at 1-800-456-6798
or business@simonandschuster.com.

Designed by Helene Berinsky

Manufactured in the United States of America

10 9 8 7 6 5 4 3 2 1

Library of Congress Cataloging-in-Publication Data is available.

ISBN 0-7432-4383-8

For my mother,
who always asks,
"What do you think she thinks?"

CONTENTS

INTRODUCTION   ix

CHAPTER ONE *Midland*   1

CHAPTER TWO *The Young Librarian*   32

CHAPTER THREE *Bush Boy*   45

CHAPTER FOUR *Motherhood and Baseball*   67

CHAPTER FIVE *The Governor's Wife*   88

CHAPTER SIX *The White House*   109

CHAPTER SEVEN *The Twins*   133

CHAPTER EIGHT *September 11*   158

CHAPTER NINE *War and Poetry*   174

ACKNOWLEDGMENTS   189

SOURCES   191

INDEX   199

INTRODUCTION

I know exactly when my fascination with Laura Bush began: when I heard that she wiped her shelves down with Clorox to relax and organized her extensive literary collection according to the Dewey decimal system.

It did not matter that these revelations caused sneering and sniping in certain quarters. The smart set of achiever women interpreted her handiwork as clear sign of compulsion and repression and even delusion, a pitiable pathology most likely caused by her marriage to a warmongering, arrogant man with less intellectual rigor than Laura herself possessed. Those smart women, were they happy?

It did not matter if this was even true. Over time, these glimpses of Laura's habits took on the power of myth. I chose to interpret them as a creation myth, and what Laura was creating for herself was a sense of serene order. She could glide through the messiest of times, composed and controlled. I wanted to figure out how she did this because I wanted some of it, too. I was an often addled woman, a decade younger than she, with three opinionated and zesty children; with fabulously messy finances and files and piles of household detritus, lost permission slips, sodden snowsuits, electronic toys, missing batteries, the works; with an exciting and funny and smart husband who couldn't put oil in the car; with a great newspaper job at a competitive and stimulating place, *The Washington Post*.

But I did not have a sense of serene order. That utterly eluded me. And when my newspaper assigned me to cover the first lady upon George W. Bush's inauguration in 2001, and I began to try to penetrate her psyche, I found myself facing situations in my own life and asking, What would Laura do? Would Laura send her daughter back upstairs to put on a shirt that covered her belly? (No.) Would Laura think it was all right to have a cigarette in the privacy of a friend's house? (Yes.) Would Laura complain about her mother-in-law? (Never overtly.)

What's so intriguing about Laura Bush is how she can be utterly familiar and, at the very same time, compellingly mysterious. Intensely bright, quietly curious, she appears wholly traditional at every milepost of her life. An only and sometimes lonely child, she decides by the second grade to be a teacher. Goes off to a conventional college for good girls, joins a sorority, plays bridge. Marries at thirty-one, fairly late for her generation, and promptly abandons her career as teacher and librarian. Cuddles the twin girls, irons the husband's shirts, weeds the flower beds, drives the car pool. Squares her shoulders and says, "Okay, dear," when he comes home and wants to move to Washington and help run Daddy's presidential campaign, wants to move to Dallas and run a baseball team, wants to move to Austin and be governor, wants to move to the White House. Never complains, ever. Through it all, she told me, a year after the attacks on the Twin Towers and the Pentagon, that she regards being the wife of George W. Bush as "the most important part of my job, whether my husband is president or not."

And yet.

There lurks this independence that seems almost subversive. Her passions are quite different from the president's; she indulges them separately, usually without any public display. Her pursuits are those of the intellectual—birding, native plants, decorative arts, art history, opera, and always, the challenging literature—and her mastery of these subjects is that of the meticulous librarian, remembering minute details, extracting themes. Intriguingly, her friends are mostly Democrats, outspoken progressives, and she has held them close for years. There are hints that her own values and private beliefs might horrify the conservative religious right so carefully courted by her husband and his political mastermind, Karl Rove.

The deal always has seemed to be this: Go off to the ballet, Laura, or read Dostoyevsky, but don't expect that George will follow. Through much of her married life, she has managed to do this delicate dance: She will have her friends and her interests, and she will support her husband expertly and never embarrass. She will campaign for other Republicans, but only sparingly, and only within the bounds of her personal integrity. During the 2002 congressional campaign, she changed a speech at the last minute to remove attacks on the candidate's opponent, a Texas Democrat she admired, whom she had worked with on education issues. Nevertheless, she showed her talents for accommodating herself to the Bush family business early on, and she's as good as any of them in the absolute loyalty department.

Once, long before George W. had any designs on the White House, Barbara Bush was complaining to a friend that her daughter-in-law Columba, the wife of Florida governor Jeb Bush, was an unpredictable ditz. "But Laura," said Bar, "now she's the one who's first lady material."

This deal of hers presents an excruciating tension, it seems to me, and requires determined sublimation. Laura manages this tension very privately. By temperament, she is modest and inclined to recede; by design, she is stubbornly protective of the small zone of privacy afforded her in this country's most visible role for a woman. She is a woman who so closely guards her inner psychological life that many dismiss her for not having one at all. Like all the Bushes in the political dynasty, with their disregard for pop psychobabble, Laura refuses to indulge publicly in examining her motivations and her choices. She won't discuss, with any depth, what shaped her character. In my interviews with her, I have always been struck by her penchant for simple sentences when talking about herself. It's a locution similar to the Dick and Jane primers she must have read to her students years ago—subject, verb, object. When I asked for her impression of George W. Bush when she first met him, she said, "I thought he was fun. I also thought he was really cute. George is very fun. He's also slightly outrageous once in a while in a very funny and fun way and I found that a lot of fun." Fun. *Five funs* in one description. But when she turns to a topic dear to her, like early childhood education or Afghan art, complex clauses tumble from her mouth, one atop the other, studded with the vocabulary one might expect from a woman who devours dense fiction. "I don't really know how to teach somebody to read," she told me the first time I interviewed her, and I remember how she straightened up in her chair and leaned forward. Her delivery quickened, and her face grew more animated. "One of the initiatives I undertook in Texas was to have a seminar for the legislature, and I brought in all the experts in early reading, who were able to relate all the latest cognitive research," she said, before plunging into a brief discourse on phonics and phonemic awareness. She knew it cold.

Does she doubt policies of her husband's administration, like the wisdom of taking information on condoms off the websites of the Centers for Disease Control or maintaining three strikes legislation for criminals? Did she weep over the destroyed antiquities of the Baghdad Museum? Does she argue in pillow talk for maintaining abortion rights? "If I differ from my husband," she once tartly told a reporter, "I'm not going to tell you." So *that's* what Laura would do, and every poll suggests the American people appreciate her for it.

But as first lady, her opportunities for intellectual debate on topics her wide reading might suggest have dried up. Her progressive friends vigorously discuss, often with disapproval, the foreign and domestic policies of the forty-third president, but they never discuss them with her. They censor themselves. "I don't know how she does it, frankly," one of her friends confided. "There's a real disconnect there, and I don't really know how she deals with it."

She deals with it with grace and uncommon placidity and an adaptability for creating a niche culture for herself that is, frankly, remarkable. And I have come to admire her for that even as I have wondered how shriveling it might be. I have watched her mold herself to what already was one of the most challenging and conflicted roles in public service, to be helpmeet and hostess and influential advocate. I have seen her smoothly show off the Christmas decorations in the historic mansion she now calls home and have listened to her as she stares out the window of her military plane, reflecting on the sadness that pierced her when she visited a Washington hospital and saw Pentagon burn victims try to salute, their stiff arms encased in bandages. I have seen her crawl around on the floor with schoolchildren—she is still most comfortable with them—and slip her hand around her husband's back, even when no cameras are there to record it. I have watched her compose her face into a grave expression when laying a wreath to commemorate the Holocaust victims at Theresienstadt, the concentration camp in the Czech Republic. I have watched her push herself into an uncharacteristic spotlight, addressing a congressional committee on education reform or giving the president's weekly radio address on rights for Afghan women, and alternately seen her react with disbelief, even after all these years, when a crowd of the Republican faithful whoops and hollers upon her entry into a crowded room. I have heard her describe how she looked out her limousine window onto the paths in Rock Creek Park in Washington soon after the inauguration, and wondered wistfully whether she might be able to walk there. The woman who has ridden remote rapids and gone birding in Belize is now confined to long walks at Camp David or in the parched scrub of Crawford.

Always, although she will not acknowledge this, she is negotiating with the expectations of the American people in what is the most bizarre volunteer job in the world. The very title is ridiculous in its mustiness—first lady—with its allusion to peerage and protocol of a much earlier era. Laura Bush hates the title. Her aides know not to use it. With women's rapid rise toward equality, the job has gotten harder, not easier. The old model of Mamie Eisenhower, who said that "Ike runs the country and I turn the lamb chops," is derided; a first lady must be substantive and work on "issues." But not too substantive: Hillary Rodham Clinton inspired seething hatred for her pushy ways. A first lady must do something. But not too much. When she was the first lady of Texas, Laura Bush assured an interviewer, "I don't do anything that I don't want to do." Which is hardly the same as saying, "I do anything I want to do." Any examination of Laura Bush's effectiveness as first lady needs to consider: Is she obligated to use all that power bestowed on her by marriage? Or does she fulfill her public duty merely by ably partnering with the leader of the free world?

She is not the woman traditionalists expect that she is, and she will not wield influence in the way modernists would like. Her conduct draws from the strong sense of self she developed long ago, long before George W. Bush came calling, in the harsh terrain of West Texas. That is where she learned to order her universe with Clorox and the Dewey decimal system. That is where the roots of Laura Welch Bush are.

THE
PERFECT
WIFE

CHAPTER ONE

❧

Midland

We feel really fortunate to have grown up in West Texas where I think values are really rock solid. It's not very easy to be pretentious. . . . West Texans will call you down immediately. I think that gave us a really solid base.

—Laura Bush, in the *Midland Star-Telegram,* September 5, 2002

She was seventeen, a few days past her birthday in her senior year, a girl with her daddy's car keys. There was a party, on a weeknight. That wasn't much the sort of thing Jenna and Harold Welch let their girl do, go to a party in the middle of the week. But really, Laura was such a good girl, this only child of theirs, an angel, a love. She had never given them a moment's trouble. She was steady and smart and quiet, and her friends were the Brownies she knew from grade school. She always laughed at her father's jokes; he was a cutup, easy and friendly and open. She always sat by her mother, though. On visits to her grandmother some hours away, Laura and her mother would take turns reading in the car out loud to each other, the huge sky of West Texas arching out before them, vast and familiar, Manifest Destiny beckoning in the shimmering of the nighttime stars.

That sky, it let you see forever. Between Midland and Lubbock, some 150 miles apart, nothing stood but a few villages and scrub and electric poles and those lonely oil pumps, dipping up, swinging down, up and down, up and down, a rhythm that gave pace and purpose to an entire region. Midland proper was so orderly, a firm societal stand against the whims and sins of the prairie. There were no bars, and dozens of churches, and the streets were testament to the disciples of commerce who had delivered the good people from a lifetime of grit and toil. Laura lived on Humble Avenue, named, transparently enough, for one of the petroleum conglomerates; the next streets over were Shell and Sinclair. That was Midland in the 1960s, the Midland that Laura's father, Harold Welch, helped to build: Your aspirations could be realized in your address— Lockheed or Cessna or Boeing avenues for the white-collar engi- neers, or Yale, Harvard, and Princeton avenues for the East Coast elites like George Herbert Walker Bush who came west to seek their fortunes in the fossils.

Those streets were laid out on a tidy grid, with millions of gal- lons of water sent to sustain lush lawns hardly native to West Texas, lawns that decades later Laura would decide were environmentally incorrect. The people in the houses liked to think they lived tidy lives—two parents, a carport, drinks at the country club, touch foot- ball after church. Beyond the town limits was untameable terrain, a flat expanse of ranchland, parched brown and ocher, unbroken by trees. You could see for miles. And it was dry, and it was clear, and it was so bright at night under the star canopy, and there wasn't traffic back in those days, not like there is today, everybody hurrying over to the Target or the Sam's Club or the Jumburrito. So there would have been no reasonable excuse for even protective parents to say no to a daughter who wanted to go to a party, especially when she was such a good and responsible girl.

And so they said yes.

And Jenna would have had her book, and Harold would have had his television, and after a spell, the phone would have rung with the news, preceded with an, "Ah'm so sorry to have to tell you . . ."

My word, she hadn't been gone but a little while, and now Laura's parents were being summoned to Midland Memorial Hospital.

Laura, they learned, had been speeding blithely out of town about 8 P.M., east on Farm Road 868, her high school friend Judy Dykes in the passenger seat. She never saw the stop sign. She never saw the other car. She plowed right through that stop sign and slammed hard into the 1962 Corvair coming south and with the right-of-way, on State Road 349, the La Mesa Highway. She was fine, really, the officer assured her parents, but bruised and banged up, and awfully upset. Judy was shaking but unharmed as well. But the boy in the other car, well, the force of the broadside impact was so severe that, well . . . He never had a chance. Michael Douglas, golden boy of Midland, high school track star, was dead on arrival at Midland Memorial Hospital. The two girls were taken there, too, in another ambulance. Mike Douglas's father had been driving another car behind his son. He saw the entire horrific scene, the explosive beginning of a nightmare that haunted him his whole life.

The front-page story in the *Midland Reporter-Telegram* was blunt and nonaccusatory. "Police said death was attributed to a broken neck," the paper reported, using that passive voice peculiar to newspaper writing. But the news flew through Midland about whose actions had caused that death.

Killing another person was a tragic, shattering error for a girl to make at seventeen. It was one of those hinges in a life, a moment when destiny shuddered, then lurched in a new direction. In its aftermath, Laura became more cautious and less spontaneous, more inclined to be compassionate, less inclined to judge another person.

What made the crash even more devastating was that the boy Laura killed was no stranger but a good friend of hers, a boy from her crowd. Some said Mike Douglas was her boyfriend. Or had been, or maybe she wanted him to be. Douglas was also a senior at Midland's Robert E. Lee High School, also seventeen. A star athlete, the kind of boy other boys wanted to be around, the kind of boy the girls sidled up to. That face and that grin stared out from the paper's front page the next day, under the headline "Lee High School Senior Dies in Traffic Mishap."

"I can see his face today," said Robert McCleskey, a contemporary of Laura's and the Bushes' personal accountant, when I interviewed him forty years later. "Always smiling. Just like his dad."

In Midland, Texas, in 1963, there were no grief counselors. No one had yet conceived of the need for such a job. And so the teenagers of Midland were at sea when it came to explaining and contemplating and coping with the shock and guilt and grief and existential angst that the young Laura Welch experienced. There were pastors who might comfort with a piece of Scripture, murmur, "Let us bow our heads in prayer," and ask for the Lord's healing power. There were parents, who might sit at the edge of their child's bed and pat a shoulder heaving with sobs. Mostly, Mike's death left his classmates stunned into silence. For most of them, and certainly for Laura, it was their first experience with someone dying young, behind the wheel. Another classmate had died a year before. Hit in the head during football practice, he was discharged from the hospital after a cursory examination, then went home and died. But with the gregarious, energetic Mike suddenly gone, the kids didn't know what to say. They didn't know what to do. They wept together at his funeral a few days later, groping toward comprehension, the girls falling apart in each other's arms, the boys stoically trudging into the Douglas home to visit the bereaved parents. "It was the first time you find you're not bulletproof and invincible," McCleskey recalled. "You don't have to deal with death. It was the first time we had to deal with all that."

Laura suffered alone. The pain was "crushing," she said years later. When all her friends went to Mike's funeral, she stayed home. Even her best friend then, who has grown to be her closest confidante, did not reach out to her. When I asked Regan Gammon, now a community activist in Austin, to recall how Laura coped with the accident, she said, "That was a very hard time. He was wonderful. It changed everyone in some way. I know I was so sad I might not have been able to see how sad Laura was. He was a very close friend of Laura's."

"Have you ever been around a high school where that sort of thing happened?" asked Tobia Hochman Gunesch, who had lived two doors down the street from Laura for much of her life and went on to become the salutatorian of Laura's graduating class. "There was a lot of high school girls' sobbing. I'm sure I never said anything directly to her, and I bet most people didn't."

High school life went on, and later that month the horror and shame that afflicted Texans from the front page of the *Midland Star-Telegram* came from the assassination of President John F. Kennedy, who had been gunned down in Dallas as he drove through town in an open Lincoln Continental. After Mike Douglas's death, Laura stayed home from school for a few weeks, and when she returned, nobody said a word about the car crash to her. The police accident report notes that the pavement was dry and the visibility excellent on the night Laura flew through the stop sign at 50 miles per hour. The photos in the police file show an intersection bisecting the flat Texas landscape, a stop sign unobscured by buildings or shrubs, nothing but utility poles marching toward the horizon. They show the violence of the impact: Mike Douglas's '62 Corvair looks like one of those carcasses police departments put by the side of the road to scare people off drinking and driving. Its metal hood and right front side panel are crumpled like a ball of paper, its entire chassis wrenched out of shape. The report by the officer on the scene notes that the investigation was not complete, but if there was any follow-up investigation, those results have long since disappeared from the files at the Midland County Attorney's Office. An air of mystery still surrounds the crash. Folks in Midland were eager to ask questions:

What was Laura doing way out of town that night? Where was she going? Who was she going to meet? But in any event, she was not charged, not even ticketed for running through the stop sign, although Douglas's death was the second fatality at that same intersection that year. The police reportedly found no evidence of drinking or excessive speed, although the report is inconclusive as to whether she was tested for alcohol. Perhaps the local authorities regarded the whole episode the same way that Laura herself described it to me, as "a tragic accident." Certainly, many of her fellow Lee students saw it that way. Perhaps, like many white teenagers of comfortable means, then and now, Laura Welch was granted that chance to make a terrible mistake without it ruining her life. Perhaps Mike Douglas's parents, who lived out in the country and weren't part of the more affluent set in town, didn't have the right connections to press for a more vigorous investigation. Perhaps they didn't have the inclination. Perhaps the powers-that-be in Midland decreed that Laura had suffered enough. Certainly when she came back to school, she was more subdued than ever. No one would have needed to ask her why.

In the 1964 *Rebelee* yearbook, the list of clubs and associations behind the name of Laura Welch is shorter than many, and longer than some. She was neither a loner nor a class leader. She was not one of those supernovas who blaze through high school. She is listed as a member of the Junior Council and a homecoming queen nominee, as well as a Student Council alternate. Some other girl became homecoming queen. The yearbook does not list her making National Honor Society for her academic achievements, or joining the Future Teachers of America, despite her current reputation as an intellectual and a girl who had devoted herself to teaching by the second grade.

Her dark hair is parted on the side, and Laura is wearing it in a bouffant flip. She is smiling in the yearbook picture; she is the prettiest girl on the page, one pleasant face in a stack of fifteen seniors, not a particularly remarkable girl. She is easy to overlook. But there is no overlooking Mike Douglas in that same yearbook. There is a two-page memoriam to him.

On the left is his senior photo, displaying his good facial bones and wide smile. On the right is a poem and two more photos, of him running in his track uniform and of him sitting in his open Jeep, the one he drove around at high school games, the one he adorned with a huge confederate flag on the frame to pay homage to the school's namesake, the Civil War's legendary Southern general Robert E. Lee.

The poem is aching and awkward, and I read it in the library of Lee High School. At the next tables lunky bored teenage boys either dozed or talked trash when the librarian was out of earshot. They wore their pants baggy, drooping below the elastic of their boxer shorts, and many had earrings. A fight broke out in the courtyard between a couple of black boys, and suddenly the library boys came to life, and ran outside to check out what was happening. They ran right past an old Civil War cannon that sat rusting in the school courtyard, the wood of its wheel spokes rotting. The bell rang just then, signaling a change of periods, and students burst into the courtyard. Fragments of noisy conversations—some in English, some in Spanish—floated on the air. "He an asshole!" a girl in a tight camisole and head wrap passionately declared to her friend. "When you gonna tell him he an asshole?" Her friend clutched her books and tossed her hair, and the pair stormed by the cannon, with its plaque saying it was dedicated by Mr. and Mrs. W. T. Douglas, in memory of their son Michael. Ancient history.

I went back inside the library. An entire glass display case had been given over to current history—the accomplishments of that once unremarkable girl, now the first lady of the United States. Here was Laura Bush in a mint-green silk suit, on the cover of *Parade* magazine, being praised for her reassuring manner after the trauma of September 11, 2001. Here was the student directory for her graduating class. I looked through the yearbook again. On the page in front of me, the poem eulogizing Mike Douglas evoked a different era, before high school violence and racial crisis and careful data chronicling the achievement gaps between the poor and middle class, before girls cussed right out loud, in the hallways, as good as the boys. Reading the poem, I could envision the yearbook adviser as the grief counselor, leaning over her student editors, in their white blouses with the Peter Pan collars, as they chewed on their pencils and struggled to eulogize their friend.

> Always I'll recall
> That sense of fun,
> The effervescent good will
> The sportsmanship.
> And—the obedience to duty
> That was Mike Douglas.
>
> . . . So—I'll close my eyes
> And remember.
> And I'll smile.

Anytime Laura Bush chooses to reminisce about her Midland roots by paging through her yearbook, Mike Douglas is forever seventeen, forever grinning, forever lithe in running shorts, forever casting a shadow over her. The serenity and strength that Americans have come to admire in their first lady are qualities hard-won. Causing Mike Douglas's death, Laura Bush told me, "made me have more of a perspective on life. And maybe I would already have had that perspective anyway. I just got it at seventeen. Certainly, as a parent, you have another perspective on a tragic accident like that. You are aware at the time, but you don't know the true implications until you have your own children.

"I grieved a lot. It was a horrible, horrible tragedy. It's a terrible feeling to be responsible for an accident. And it was horrible for all of us to lose him, especially since he was so young," she said in an interview with *Oprah* magazine. "But at some point I had to accept that death is a part of life, and as tragic as losing Mike was, there was nothing anyone could do to change that. . . . It was a comeuppance. At that age, you think you're immortal, invincible. You never expect to lose anybody you love when you're so young. For all of us, it was a shock. It was a sign of the preciousness of life and how fleeting it can be."

It is a few days after the Grand Old Party's triumphant sweep on election day 2002, and the ladies of the Midland County Republican Women's club have put on their knit suits and their star-spangled elephant pins and flocked to their monthly luncheon upstairs at the Petroleum Club. The Petroleum Club is a bulwark of old Midland, which is a town where, everyone tells you, everyone knows everybody else. As always, this is not exactly right. Old Midland tries to stand firm. There is the Petroleum Club, and the First United Methodist Church—"Sharing Christ from the Heart of Midland"— and the Young Men's Christian Association up on Big Spring Road, and Johnny's Barbecue, where Laura's daddy, Harold Welch, used to put down his friendly wagers on football Saturdays. Harold died in 1995, and now his contemporaries stay away from the hot sauce and plant themselves in front of Johnny's small TV to stare as their stocks crawl across the bottom of CNBC. And much of downtown Midland is abandoned. Its storefronts are vacant. There's no department store anymore. Oil Bust is writ on every city block. From far away on the flatlands, driving toward Midland some twenty miles out, you can see the tall buildings glistening in the distance, like Oz. But when you get up close, they're mostly empty.

The old Ritz Theater doesn't show movies anymore, but it's kept alive with salsa nights on Tuesdays. Everybody doesn't know everybody else because the people frequenting salsa night at the old theater are working the dishwasher at the Petroleum Club, not sitting down in the dining room. Once, only the oilmen, the engineers and the independent operators and the map men held court at the Petroleum Club, gathering each day promptly at noon for food and drinks and cards at a penny a hand. Once, only Democrats populated West Texas, and Republicans were considered, as George W. Bush once said, "kind of weird." Change comes little by little, even to Midland. The oilmen are still downstairs at the Petroleum Club, but now the Republican ladies drift upstairs to lunch, clouds of perfume and tinkly laughter trailing down the stairs behind them.

The room is full. The Midland Republican Women are a force, capital *F,* and state officials have learned to come pay their due, since George W.'s father, George Herbert Walker Bush, nearly single-handledly muscled the GOP into the state. Laura's mother, Jenna Welch, is there, sitting at a table near the dais, and various ladies come to pay their respects. She is much loved, and she gets around quite ably, Jenna does, for a woman born in 1919. She lives alone in the house on Humble Avenue and drives herself around town, to meetings and church and Tuesday suppers at Luby's Cafeteria, where her adult Bible study group has been eating weekly for years. ("Of all the Bible groups," the pastor of First United Methodist Church of Midland, C. Lane Boyd, told me, "Jenna's group has the most fun.") Or she's running down to Austin for the book festival her daughter started, or she's flying off to meet up with her at the White House or the Crawford ranch. She has persevered through widowhood and breast cancer and the plummet of her retirement stock with Enron. That last hurdle came to the world's attention when President Bush declared publicly, in indignation, "even my mother-in-law lost $7,000," which caused Jenna to chide him, "That's the last time I tell you anything about my investments." Jenna was a Democrat until she became a Republican-in-law. But she and Harold were never "one of those yellow-dog democrats, you know, would rather vote for a yellow-dog than a Republican," her son-in-law, the president, has said. "They weren't, you know, un*reasonable* Democrats." That was his wife, Laura, who voted for Eugene McCarthy.

After everybody moves through the buffet line, getting some ham and green beans, the incoming president of the Midland County Republican Women, Beverly Brock, rises to speak. She looks quite a bit like Tammy Faye Bakker, and she invokes how God helped Texas Republicans to a magnificent win in the previous week, sweeping the offices of governor and lieutenant governor and U.S. senator and on down. Denise Burns, who is the wife of former Midland mayor Bobby Burns, whispers to me: "Do you think God's on our side? I don't think God's a Republican or a Democrat." The audience of a couple hundred of these faithful is a sea of red, white, and blue, and Bobby surveys the women, then smiles and drawls: "If you got them against you, you got a problem." Today, the gossip of those in charge of Midland is over what prompted their congressman to abruptly announce his resignation, only days after he had won a new term. Jockeying for his position has already begun, and Beverly Brock addresses this new political opportunity by saying, to the Midland County Republican Women, "we have a lot of good men available to us," to seek the seat. To me, the Yankee, the Easterner, this seems a startling oversight with so many accomplished women in earshot, including the outgoing president, who is one of the town's assistant district attorneys. And Denise Burns notes it as well. This very morning her husband has been on the local television station to smoothly reference his own prospects, but now Denise says, with a laugh, "Maybe *I'll* do it. You can stay here and watch him play football," referring to their high-schooler son. Denise is in her forties, and she works in Bobby's insurance agency.

Then David Dewhurst, impossibly tall, smelling of cologne, hair overcoiffed, speaks to the ladies. He has just ascended to lieutenant governor, which some say is the executive spot in Texas with the real authority, more power than the governor has. He pledges there will be a state income tax "over my cold dead body." He promises to cut the "unacceptable" high school dropout rate, which floats between a shocking 30 and 50 percent. The ladies burst into applause. They pass the ceramic elephant bowls to raise some funds for operations, and Jenna snaps open the clasp of her handbag and removes a few bills. She is wearing a very nice royal blue knit suit, and it sets off her eyes. To look at her is to see the source of her daughter's sense of grace. To look at the entire scene is to see the source of her daughter's sense of where women fit into the world.

Later that night, I sit down for dinner at the Greentree Country Club with Steve Buck, who is the president of the Midland Federation of Teachers, and I tell him about my visit with the Republican ladies, which he readily interprets. His own attitudes toward race and class and gender began to change when he got out of town after high school and went to North Texas State, which actually had black athletes, and when he started teaching, and got to know women.

"Not only was Midland prejudiced against color, no oil company ever hired a female," he says. "I mean, I don't think there was an engineer who was female or working in any way, other than a secretary, ever. I mean, that was just the good ol' boys. And the oil deals were done at bars and clubs. They were all done on a handshake. Women were not allowed. And that's the reason why, those women at the Republican Women's club, they have never worked a day in their lives. Not one day. That's why they can have their meetings at noon on a Wednesday. But they can all sit right there and write out of their checking accounts, big, big checks."

"They've got their Junior League on Thursday," adds Steve's wife, Peggy, also a teacher. "And Garden Club on Friday."

"And that is still what they do," says Steve. "That's the role of women here. And that has a lot to do with why Laura is the way she is, too. She was brought up in that role for women."

Laura herself has said, "I've always done what really traditional women do, and I've been very, very satisfied."

Not that that's the whole story. It never is. People who look uncomplicated may instead be preternaturally disciplined, or disinclined to reveal their complications in public.

Laura Lane Welch was born in Midland on November 4, 1946, as the post–World War II boom watered the parched Permian Basin with money. More Texan than her husband, with his New England pedigree, she doesn't much talk about "her people," and there is no detail of her early years on her official White House biography. Doing what "really traditional women do" means selling short those years before your marriage. But in the foreword to *Whatever the Wind Delivers*, a collection of archival photos and poetry of West Texas, Laura writes that the book "could be a scrapbook from my father's side of the family. My grandparents, Mark and Lula Lane Welch, moved to Lubbock in 1918, and that's where they stayed. They lived through the 'dust bowl' days, and these images might have been familiar to them. My father, Harold Welch, was six when they arrived." The black-and-white photographs in the book evoke a frontier land of hardened, sunburned men and the tough women, sturdy of temperament, they found to accompany them. There are women in good long white dresses, posing before covered wagons, defiant apostles for maintaining proper ways in the face of harsh conditions. There is a tiny child perched atop a huge swaybacked workhorse, and a remarkable captured moment of leisure in all that hard life—women in bonnets and men in scuffed boots doing a two-step procession, making their own fun, far from any organized entertainment. Her ancestors sank their roots into Laura Bush that way. She has that same capacity for creating a sense of place and community out of the harshest conditions of her own.

In the collection's foreword, Laura said she had been fascinated with West Texas since her early trips to Lubbock. As a reflective adult, she came to understand, "To survive, every day is a negotiation, an agreement, an acceptance of terms that the soil and the sky outline without the slightest bit of consideration. And yet, even at its worst—at its dustiest, hottest, and driest—the region is rich with anticipation and hope for a merciful change. And it does change.

"Just when a man resigns his fields to a dry season, precious rain bursts from a cloud, calming the dust about his boots, washing the red dirt off the windows of his pickup and summoning birds to bathe and drink. This is the paradox of West Texas and the mighty Southwest. It is at once dull and unpredictable; subtle and grand." It is impossible to read these words without seeing them as metaphor— no, as actual premonition—for the paradox of a wife's life within 1600 Pennsylvania Avenue, at once constrained and lavish with opportunity.

Laura Bush comes from stalwart maternal stock, a line of women who adapted themselves to heartbreak and deprivation. "Texas is a pretty unforgiving landscape," Laura said, "and it was a difficult state for women as well as for men. I think that's one reason Texas is known for having so many strong women." An only child, Laura was born to an only child. Jenna Welch's mother, Jessie, was one of seven girls, raised alone by their mother, Laura's great-grandmother Eva, after her husband committed suicide and left her a widow at forty-two. According to Jenna Welch, Eva maintained a successful dairy farm outside Little Rock, Arkansas, using her own girls as the labor, for the milking and barn cleaning and delivery. They were independent women, all of them, in the only way that was acceptable—earning their livelihood. If Eva had still had a husband, her business acumen would have been considered uppity. But she was alone, and her independence therefore acceptable to the social structure, although it might have been seen as a quality to be pitied rather than admired. Her daughter Jessie, Laura's maternal grandmother, made the milk deliveries in a Model T. Along the way, she met a postman. The milkwoman and the mailman came from the same kind of family. Harold Hawkins also had been raised by a widow, who provided for her five children by running the family grocery store. They got married, and when Harold joined the army in World War I, Jessie Hawkins took over her husband's mail route. When Laura visited them at their home in El Paso when she was little, her granddaddy would sometimes sip Texas Select bourbon instead of orange juice in the morning. Her grandmother loved her gardening, and died doing just that.

With that formidable matriarchy behind her, Jenna Hawkins, Laura's mother, maintained her own flinty but quiet independence after her marriage to Harold Welch, who hitched her up at the Fort Bliss military chapel during one of his army leaves in 1944. After the war, Welch worked for a credit company in El Paso, but he wanted to be a home builder the way his father had been in Lubbock. He and Jenna moved to Midland, named for its location halfway between El Paso and Dallas, to build homes for workers in the burgeoning oil business. He developed scores of individual homes around town. He and Jenna were a team. He built; she kept the books. "Mrs. Welch helped run the financial part of that business," said Robert McCleskey. "She was pretty sharp with investments and stuff like that." Harold was garrulous and charismatic, always quick with a slap on the back and a quip. Jenna was reserved and refined and delighted in her husband's humor. Their only child watched that marriage and took it as a model for her own, and noted: Jenna was a woman "of that generation who really wanted to please her husband and cooked three meals a day. . . . But she was also interested in a lot of things outside her marriage." Jessie had passed down to her daughter a keen interest in the natural world—Jenna could name and identify hundreds of birds and plants native to the region—and she in turn passed this down to her daughter. When Jenna was the Girl Scout troop leader and shepherded the girls toward their badges, she made sure those girls could identify their Texas birds.

Bird-watching is easily dismissed as fusty by those enamored of louder, action-packed pursuits. It is the essence of passive passion, and, if humans were catalogued in the way Audubon did birds, their entry might read, "Bird-watchers most often are observed in the company of readers, knitters, crossword puzzlers, and fanciers of other solitary, meditative pursuits." It is contemplative and sooth- ing, and, to those reflective souls seeking to learn some subtleties of the vast social hierarchy of nature, it could be revealing. Jenna was particularly found of the phalarope, a water bird. She once noted that "the female runs off on little errands of her own, and leaves the male to care for the young." When it came to birding, neither Harold Welch nor George Bush could be bothered. In Bush's case, the image of him sitting for hours without moving was flat-out ridiculous, a man who lived for speed—fighter jets, cigarette racer boats, the six-minute mile. But he would indulge his wife's natural- ist habits, even showing off to visitors at their Crawford ranch the stands of hardwoods they preserved as habitat for the rare golden- cheeked warbler.

In a precious few generations, West Texas life had grown con- siderably easier for the Hawkins women. But Jenna had her sor- rows. She miscarried several times. Over and over, she carried a baby nearly to term, only to go into labor prematurely and have the baby die within days. Laura was certainly aware of her parents' painful quest for more children. Once, they told her they were look- ing for a little brother or sister for her, and took her along for a visit to the Gladney adoption home in Fort Worth, although they later decided not to continue with the adoption. And Laura at an early age began feeling some responsibility for her parents' emotional well-being, much like her husband, George, who at the age of seven took on the role of caring for his mother, Barbara, after the death of his sister Robin. "I felt very obligated to my parents," Laura said. "I didn't want to upset them in any way."

And she grew up "sort of lonely," she said, although she was always careful to add what an idyllic childhood she had in 1950s and 1960s Midland, where nobody ever locked their doors and kids pedaled everywhere on their bikes. Her parents doted on her. Jenna knew from her own experience that being an only child could bind you closely to your mother. It could confer unparalleled self-assurance. Only children don't need to compete for their parents' love and attention; it flows solely to them. But they are also deprived of the steadfast fraternity of siblings. Jenna put Laura in dance classes and Brownies and choir at First United Methodist Church and swimming lessons. It was quite the scheduled life for a child of that era in small-town Texas. The little girl was so eager for friends that after her first week of private kindergarten, she had memorized the name of every student in her class. Looking back, Laura said, "I was lucky to have a very normal childhood in a small town where people felt very free to do whatever we wanted to do. We were sheltered in this freedom in a way that maybe we didn't understand."

Laura herself and many of her friends recollect the Midland of their youth as a rosy world of slumber parties and recess games and sodas at the Rexall drugstore. Summers, boys played baseball, and girls splashed around in each other's pools. In important ways, though, this freedom was reserved for a special group—the white offspring of the middle class. Midland was segregated; its school district was among the last, and, according to some accounts, dead last in the nation to be integrated, and even then only when the federal government threatened to bring in the marshals. Blacks lived on the other side of Florida Avenue, and knew to stay in their place, the women venturing out only to work as domestics for the white ladies. Hispanics were "wetbacks," who had been smuggled in to pick cotton. And women? They were to keep to their place, too.

Jenna Welch had been smart enough to marry a man who respected her mind and let her put it to use. Behind the carefully tended lawns and solid brick walls of their houses, many intelligent women drank their boredom away. Dottie Craig remembers them well.

The geographic isolation of Midland was especially severe for the transplants, women from back East whose husbands decided to strike it rich in the Permian Basin. The daughter of a New York city surgeon and a Phi Beta Kappa graduate of Vassar College, Dottie Craig has lived in Midland for more than fifty years. She can still remember vividly that August day in 1950 when her husband, Earle, returned from his reconnaissance of Midland to the lush rolling hills of western Pennsylvania, where they lived. Dottie said she asked Earle, " 'What is Midland like?' And he said, 'There's a town nearby called No Trees,' and I nodded, and then I went out in the garden and I cried."

Like George and Barbara Bush, with whom they became close friends, the Craigs came from old moneyed families, but Earle felt compelled to prove himself on his own. He had taken flight training in Texas during World War II, "and I thought it would be glamorous to come back and engage in the oil and gas business, so I did."

"And has it been glamorous for you?" I ask him, and Dottie gives a sardonic laugh. But Earle says, "Yes, now and then, and there's a lot of ups, and there have been a lot of downs." The Craigs have invited me to their home, and, although it is the middle of a weekday, Earle is wearing a pink dress shirt with cuff links. Dottie is wearing Ferragamo shoes and black slacks and a dusty blue sweater. She is lovely and elegant, with white hair and hip glasses, a displaced WASP in the grit of West Texas. Bloom where you're planted and all that, but thank God they keep the apartment in Manhattan and the home in Nantucket.

When they arrived in Midland in 1950, says Earle, "It was one of the worst droughts of the century, and we frequently had sandstorms where literally you could just barely see across the street."

And Dottie adds, "You could write your name in dust on the dining room table. We didn't have a dryer. And we had a baby. And I can remember my neighbor calling me because she had lived in Midland much longer than me, to let me know that a sandstorm was coming and I had to rush and get my diapers off the laundry line." Their parents thought they were real frontier people. Her father, the doctor, thought her baby would be delivered by an Indian squaw, and he was only partially joking.

Dottie Craig wasn't the only one who cried. Even women from other parts of Texas found Midland forbidding. Lynn Munn, a friend of Laura's who grew up in Dallas, remembers coming home from grocery shopping one day, her two small children in tow, and finding a tumbleweed "the size of a Volkswagen Beetle" blocking her front door. She burst into tears. Mary Ann Ryerson, who grew up with Laura, said her mother wept through the entire first year she lived in Midland, after moving away from the water of Corpus Christi.

Such rugged conditions certainly fostered bonds. Women could trade tips on how best to get dust out of the house, and Lord, that alone could be a full-time job. Hearing these stories, I began to think that Laura Bush's shelf-Cloroxing was less compulsive than pragmatic. The dirt and the wind and the heat and the dryness that bake your skin and make your throat ache, the lack of shade, and above all else, the isolation all conspire to make West Texans a breed apart. When I asked Robert McCleskey if Midlanders were different, he leaned back in his wooden office chair and considered. "Oh, wellllll, I guess," he drawled. "We don't have trees, and we don't have water. We don't know how to swim, and we can't climb a tree. That makes us different."

Folks were, and are, friendly to most outsiders and quick to engage them in conversation. They're eager to have someone new bring them stories of some other place. In Midland, when somebody asks "How ya dewin?," answering "Okay" is considered impolite. It tags you as ignorant at best, stuck-up at worst. The proper answer always is: "I'm doing fine, thank you for asking. How *you* dewin?" It is an exchange that typifies a culture of conversation and caring for each other. Folks in Midland reserve their fiercest loyalty for each other. They know each other, and protect each other, and comfort each other, and each other's kin. Despite racial divides, there is a continuity through the town and a way of papering over any real conflicts with politeness. Like those pioneers dancing in front of the covered wagon in the nineteenth century, Midlanders have to make their own fun and tend to their own troubles, be it the drought that kills the cattle or the well that goes dry or the entire oil economy that sputters to a halt. You can never count on the money, although the giddy tried, and left a trail of foreclosed houses, repossessed Rolls-Royces, planes, and yachts behind them. Often, a man's financial failure is perceived as having nothing to do with his business acumen. No, a man can go from boom to bust and back again, yanked about by forces completely outside his control. Life can be an accident of luck or disaster, Midland tells itself, and the only dependable elements are families and friends and the Lord.

To this day, Laura Bush's closest friends are the women she knew in grade school—Regan Gammon, Jan O'Neill, Peggy Porter Weiss, Marge Petty, Jane Ann Fontenot. There wasn't much for girls in the small-town Texas culture that formed them. Elsewhere in America, during Laura's high school years, women were agitating for equality. But in Midland, the 1964 *Rebelee* yearbook reflects the same old restricted paths for women. An article about the separate but equal vocational training for the genders is headlined "Future Wives, Shop Students Try Special Schools." And the accompanying photograph bears the caption: "Home Ec girls, realizing the way to their future husbands' hearts, try out their cooking skills." Laura wasn't in that picture, but Jenna Welch, remembering her only child's early years, dutifully recalled, "She liked to cook, as all little girls do." In Laura's years of high school, girls primped and lay around on each other's beds, "listening to Ricky Nelson records," said Tobia Gunesch. There were many occasions that called for white gloves. They are in pictures in the *Rebelee* yearbook, at prom and cotillion and various debutante events. Life has changed for girls in Midland today, but there still isn't anything they can do that gets the 20,000 people screaming under the Friday night lights of high school football season. Except be a cheerleader, in service to the quarterback.

As first lady, Laura Bush is often portrayed as the more compassionate and emotionally nuanced partner in the White House. Her quieter, more reflective mien is served up to soften George Bush's sharper retorts, his quick judgments, his black-and-white morality. His critics portray him as overly arrogant, even swaggering, in the surety with which he declares his mission, especially in the area of foreign policy. Laura is seen as reining him in. When he evoked the Wild West with his insistence that Osama bin Laden would be brought in "dead or alive," Laura sidled up to her husband and said pointedly, if softly, "Bushie, are you gonna git 'em?" This was her way of toning down his Texas cowboy rhetoric, reminding him how poorly it would play across the nation. In point of fact, though, Laura is the one with the real Texas credo, much more of a product of Midland and its ethos than her husband, who was sent to prep school in Connecticut and summered on the craggy Maine coast among the old-moneyed families.

It takes about fifteen minutes to drive from what somebody with some swagger named the Midland International Airport and into downtown. In that time, you can place your unborn baby or come to Jesus or pawn your valuables, as instructed by the billboards along Highway 20. Back when Laura was growing up in the modest three-bedroom rancher on Humble Avenue where her mother still lives, folks liked to say that you raised hell in Odessa, but you raised your family in Midland. Over and over, when Laura and her girlfriends have obliged interviewers with an account of their upbringing, they mention the same things: the freedom they had as children and teenagers; the simplicity of routine; the love they felt from community. In this version of the town's life, "You were free to ride your bike anywhere and go all around town by yourself," Laura said, and she and Regan and Peggy would pedal over to the Rexall drugstore for cherry Cokes. In high school, the girls would pile into one car and stop by Agnes's, one of the local drive-ins. "There were at least five girls in the car every time we went out cruising," said Peggy Porter Weiss, who now owns an of-the-moment restaurant in Austin. "We liked Kent cigarettes and would be down on the floor in the back of the car smoking." In this carefully pruned tale of conventional girlhood, there were the slumber parties and the dancing around the room in sock feet. Laura loved to dance, and she had lots of records. When Regan got a copy of *Meet the Beatles*, "we played that album over and over again," says Weiss. "Regan liked Paul, I liked John, and I think Laura liked all of them."

There were three movie theaters downtown, and three drive-ins, and the teenagers went to those drive-ins a lot on double dates. Sometimes, they would sneak in beer. "If you had a cheapskate date, he would put you in the trunk," recalls Ryerson, to avoid the price of a ticket. The biggest concern was "making sure your mom didn't smell your vodka breath," says Gunesch.

"You didn't hear about anything terribly wild," says Ryerson. "Boys would go to Mexico and find some whorehouses over the border. And since Midland was dry, you had to go to Odessa, find somebody's older brother to be your rum-runner. But there was always a way—I remember one spot where you were supposed to be able to buy beer with your library card."

And life in Midland in the 1960s seemed freed of the strictures of, if not race, certainly of status and class and money. The oil roughnecks and laborers lived over there in hard-drinking Odessa, leaving Midland proper for the operators and engineers and those who supported the business side of the oil and gas industry—the insurance agents, the draftsmen, the merchants, the car dealers, the home builders. Kids ran in different packs, but their boundaries seemed permeable. You might not be in the most popular group, but you would be invited along to the party just the same.

"Midland had a definite little hierarchy," said Jane Fontenot, now a certified nurse midwife in Berkeley, California. Their group "was a little bit more studious, but we weren't the real brainy group. Our little group was just not quite as anxious to fit in and be that popular. We were a little bit more out there, a little bit more adventurous and experimental."

Laura was one of the popular girls who dated a lot, "kind of a late bloomer type, I guess," says McCleskey, who went to Midland High. "You know, there were always a few girls you went to school with, didn't pay attention to, and one day you looked up and said, Damn! Where'd she come from! Where'd she been?

"You knew everybody from church, or we boys bumped into each other playing ball in the summer," adds McCleskey, who has been eating lunch with the same group of men going on thirty years. When he was young, the accountant never sorted people by their financial assets. Even the swimming pool, that most delicious of accoutrements, seemed sorted by gender rather than affordability. "The girls seemed to have the pools. For some reason, the boys didn't," he recalled. "Not everybody had cars. In our generation, I can still remember when my folks became a two-car family, and I can remember thinking, 'Boy, we must've made it.' I remember my mother driving downtown to drop my father off to work, and picking him back up in the evening. If you wanted the car, that was what you had to do."

Money didn't really matter among their set that had some, because no matter how much of it you had, there was nothing to do anyway but go to the movies or ride lazily around sneaking smokes or spin records in each other's rec rooms. "You never really knew who had it or not," recalls Ryerson. "Probably our parents knew.

You really didn't think about it. You didn't really even know what anybody's parents did. It wasn't that big a deal. My dad was in the oil business and lived below his means because he came from the Depression, and he knew it was feast or famine in the oil business. I can remember during the boom years of the 1980s, coming back home and hearing him tell me, 'These people buying Mercedeses now—they're going to be sorry.'

"There was just nothing to do, so it wasn't like money kept you out or in."

In a way that sounds almost false in this status-conscious time, Midland kids really did like each other for who they were, rather than what they had. It was "remarkable because there was so little to do. Personal relationships took on more importance," said Fontenot. "Perhaps that's why people are so loyal to each other." They had grown up knowing each other all their lives, and even now, the ones who left because of the town's smallness and isolation still yearn for its sense of community. Of her girlhood, says Laura herself, "Mostly, I think I remember a feeling of being really sheltered."

There was certainly trouble in the world, but that news seemed so far away, so removed from life at Lee High School. In the beginning of November 1963, the *Midland Reporter-Telegram*, which cost 5 cents, carried front-page stories about the assassination of the president of South Vietnam and his brother and a freak accident in Indianapolis that had killed sixty-two watching an ice show at the local fairgrounds. "An explosion hurled flames and concrete slabs as large as pianos" through the watching crowd, the story said, and "bodies, many still wrapped in mink, erupted onto the ice." And at least once a week, there were stories about the gas and oil industry that are unintelligible to the outsider but not the oil and gas men who smoked their cigarettes and played their bid whist at the Petroleum Club: "Socony Mobil Oil Company Inc. No. 1 George K. Mitchell Terrell County Prospect 29 miles north of Dryden is testing the upper and lower Strawn through perforations. Earlier, the lower Strawn section at 11,630-670 feet had flowed gas the max rate of 3 million cubic feet daily, through a 1/2 inch choke for an unreported period of time."

On the day the newspaper listed the pallbearers for the funeral of Michael Douglas, it also carried a story many in Midland found more ominous: The University of Texas regents had voted unanimously to integrate college athletics, the first Southwest Conference school to do so. The ruling was "to remove all student restrictions of every kind and character based on race or color."

What Laura Bush never mentions in her accounts of growing up in Midland—not in interviews nor in all the speeches she has given as first lady of Texas and the United States to commemorate Martin Luther King Day—is that she grew up in a time and place where segregation ruled completely. Many politicians reach back to their upbringing and excavate some detail of discord that propelled them to action. George Bush doesn't call upon Midland in that way, and neither does Laura. For them, Midland is always that place where people had only good values. It is an odd view of America, to look back on this town and see it as a paradise without mentioning this shame. In those tales of high school hijinks at Agnes's Drive-In, no one mentions that Agnes was a stubborn old racist woman, who never let blacks near her business. The history of race and bias in Texas may seem well worn now, but its grip on Midland is uglier and more persistent than elsewhere. Even now, the Ku Klux Klan likes to boast that it gets plenty of financial support from dependable members in Midland. Even now, some people look away, their mouths tightening with disapproval, when they see an interracial couple holding hands on the street. Even now, the race wars of the 1960s are still being fought, this time in political resistance to bond issues that would add funds for a school district that is now more than 50 percent black and Hispanic.

For Laura and her friends growing up, brown people and black people seemed nonexistent. They seemed invisible. "I went off to Stanford, and I remember people saying, 'Oh, you must be prejudiced, you're from Texas, you must not like black people,'" recalls Mary Ann Ryerson, who went to Lee with Laura and later became a bilingual teacher in the Houston school district. "And I would say, 'Oh, gosh, I don't really *know* any.' The only person you knew was your maid. And some people had a Hispanic maid and some people had a black maid. And the caddies at the country club, who were all black. At Lee High School, I don't even think there were any Hispanics. They were at Midland High." At Stanford, she came across strident students working to register blacks as part of the Student Nonviolent Coordinating Committee, SNCC, and was amazed. "It was a whole new world," she says.

Steve Buck remembers working during high school to hire wetbacks—"that's just what we called them then, before we knew better," he says—to pick cotton. "In fact, in my first job, I made more money in high school in Midland, Texas, than I did my first few years of school teaching, because there was so much more money out here. If you could speak a little bit of Spanish, you could get eight or ten of them to come work for you, and you'd hire them out to the farmer and he'd pay and you were the middle guy—you'd make money. We were all doing that in high school. They couldn't line up work otherwise. I was sixteen, and one summer, I had about fifteen of them working for me at one time. And I was paying them seventy cents an hour, and I was charging the farmer ninety cents. So I was making 20 cents off each one of them per hour. You know, you would never think about doing that today. But in those days, that was kind of the deal."

When he graduated from Lee High School in 1969 and went to the University of North Texas, "that was the first time I'd ever seen a black in school or been around a black. And I remember I didn't know what to call them properly. Out here, everybody had five or six different names for blacks. You had niggers, you had nigras, you had coloreds, you had colored boys—and then I got over to college and I heard the term for the first time—Afro-American. But in the 1960s, Midland was not even like the rest of the South. A lot of places, even in Fort Worth, might have a colored section, colored water fountains, colored restrooms. Not in Midland. You had nothing. They just did not eat in restaurants," he said. The 1968 Olympics in Mexico City were memorable to those in Midland not for John Carlos and Tommie Smith and their black power salute on the medal stand, but because Midland native Doug Russell beat out Mark Spitz to win the gold medal in the 100-meter butterfly.

But the adults of Midland had noticed warily what was going on, and plenty of them had complained and resisted. In the voting booth, they defeated civil rights supporter Lyndon Baines Johnson every single time he appeared on the ballot. When Laura Welch and George W. Bush were attending San Jacinto Junior High School, a social studies teacher quit his job to run against Johnson for the U.S. Senate. He told his students he just couldn't stand by and "let LBJ ruin Texas." Such sentiment was not uncommon in the classroom among those charged with imparting civic values to youth. When the schools were finally integrated, fifteen years after *Brown v. Board of Education* struck down public school segregation, black students filed into Laura Welch's alma mater. Laura was in Houston, in her first year of teaching in a poor school. And back at Lee, one teacher took five desks and turned them toward the back wall of her classroom. She told her black students, "They told me I had to have you in here, but they didn't tell me I had to look at you."

On that afternoon when Lee Harvey Oswald climbed the stairs of the Texas Book Depository and took aim at President Kennedy, the usual crowd of businessmen and luncheoning ladies filled the dining room at Luigi's, one of the only fine restaurants in Midland at that time. Its owner heard the news crackle over the radio. Horrified, he figured he had an obligation to share the tragic report with his patrons. Over the public address system, he announced, "Ladies and gentlemen, the president of the United States has just been shot and seriously wounded in Dallas." There was a second of silence while the news registered, and then the diners burst into applause.

In this regard, George Bush, for all his claim to his roots in Texas, was growing up differently. The word *nigger* was not tolerated at his home; Barbara Bush once grew red with anger and smacked him when she heard him toss the term off to a bunch of his boyhood pals. And Bar did not restrict her ban on such language to her own domain. Earle and Dottie Craig, the well-bred immigrants, remember her confronting one of Midland's social stalwarts. "It was sewing circle," said Dottie. "One of the senior local ladies used the unforgivable word in front of a black servant in Bar's house," said Earle, "and Bar excoriated that woman, who was senior to her: 'Never. Do. That. Again.' "

"Bar really would not put up with that sort of thing," said Dottie, "which is very common in the South and isn't considered as objectionable as it is to those of us who grew up in the East."

The black population of Midland is and was small. During the 1960s, when the town had a population of about fifty thousand, perhaps five thousand blacks lived in the neighborhoods south of Florida Avenue. When I called to set up an appointment with Dr. Viola Coleman, a proud and determined physician still practicing in her eighties, who led the fight to desegregate the schools, she told me wryly: "Now, I'm black, so you *know* I live on the other side of the tracks." As I talked with other people around Midland, who were unfailingly helpful with questions about Laura, they always would ask where else I had been. And when I told them I had been over on Florida Avenue, their eyes would widen, and they would wonder what in heaven's name I could have been doing over there. Or they would look at me quizzically when I mentioned the spanking new Supermercado, with its tortilleria baking fresh tortillas daily on the premises and its shelves studded with calabaza and mangoes. It was a huge place, with bright purple and yellow walls, over past Big Spring Highway, but many in Midland seemed to have never noticed it, let alone gone inside. When I mentioned this to Dr. Coleman, she just smiled. "Even today, there are people who don't know there is anything past Big Spring," she said of the neighborhoods west of the highway, where the youngster George Bush once lived with his parents, that are now primarily Hispanic. "It is a community that remains invisible."

The adamant resistance to integration and civil rights was all the more remarkable in Midland because the small black population was generally undemanding. It was understood that black women would work in white women's homes, "seven days a week, cooking three meals a day," said Dr. Coleman, "and you went to church on Sunday evenings, because that was when you got to finally come home." The unrest—the cross burnings and marches and riots that raced through the Deep South—passed Midland by. Life for blacks centered around church and school just as it did for whites. George Washington Carver High School had its own fine marching band, its own football team, its own academic elites. As in much of the rest of America, segregation in Midland did impose a social structure on the black neighborhood. Unable to live and work among whites, black doctors and lawyers and restaurant and business owners became pillars of the local black community. And when some of those leaders finally began organizing a sit-in at a few of Midland's favorite lunch spots, the town's white business community was so eager to avert the spectacle of such an action that the restaurant owners, except for Agnes, quietly agreed to open their doors to blacks. And that was that. One day, Mary Ann Ryerson remembers, she and her mother were eating at Fuhr's cafeteria. And Mary Ann's mother whispered to her, "Look, some blacks are eating over there," at a nearby table. The girl nodded, a bit surprised. She had never noticed when black folks weren't eating at Fuhr's, and now she hadn't noticed when they were.

Of course, Laura and many of her contemporaries moved beyond

Midland and its myopic view of minorities. By the time she went looking for work as a school librarian in Austin, Laura deliberately chose schools where she could serve a decidedly disadvantaged population of poor minority children. But as adults, her generation held on to the way they had related in high school. When Laura and George Bush hosted her high school class reunion at the Governor's Mansion in Austin in 1997, they threw open their doors to Laura's fellow graduates of Lee High School as well as to the members of the 1964 class of Midland High. Some five hundred people ate barbecue and drank Lone Star beer and twisted the night away, marveling how far the pretty girl with the twinkly smile had come. Nobody even thought to invite the members of the class of 1964 of Midland's third high school, all-black George Washington Carver. "Nobody even *remembered*," said someone who attended. "Isn't that incredible? Isn't that awful?"

After that final and traumatic year at Lee High School, punctured by the deadly and permanent consequences of a split-second error in judgment and the shocking assassination of a president, Laura Lane Welch left Midland behind. She was an only child who had grown self-assured. Her father, who made her laugh, and her mother, who tended her mind, had given her unconditional love, the most important quality parents can bestow upon a child, because it is the bedrock of self-confidence. She was the center of their attention without even having had to seek it, and that assurance would define all her subsequent relationships. Already, Laura had developed the reserve that made her difficult to describe. To casual acquaintances, her temperament seemed unremarkable. Years later, they would struggle to quantify her, and she would somehow elude them. They would say, with an apologetic shrug, "Laura is just Laura." She was not boring, or bland, but stable, and her natural tendency toward quietude had deepened after the fatal accident. She became a keen and careful listener, and friends would be taken aback when she brought up a fragment of something they had told her months before.

The Midland spirit "really has something to do with the landscape because the sky is so huge. There is a real feeling of unlimited possibilities here," she said, noting that the capricious oil business attracted risk-takers and optimists. But if the town sheltered her as a girl, it hemmed her in as a young woman. She would live in Houston and Dallas and Austin, and travel for weeks through Europe, growing more curious and questioning and opinionated with each successive year. And then, nearly fifteen years later, she would suddenly abandon her career and return, to construct for herself the conventional life of an upper-middle-class woman in Midland—marriage, motherhood, housekeeping, charity work. If not for the outsized political aspirations of her husband, Laura Bush might be there still, and perfectly satisfied. Instead, her life underwent a startling transformation.

CHAPTER TWO

The Young Librarian

I know you don't hear often enough how much we appreciate you. I know,
because I've been there.

— Laura Bush, praising teachers in a 2001 speech

The little girl who had memorized the names of all her kindergarten classmates in the first week fixed on the notion of
teaching quite early on. She adored her second-grade teacher,
Charlene Gnagy, and she decided she would be a teacher, too. Content to amuse herself for long periods of time, Laura Welch would
play school, lining up her dolls and lecturing them. One day, when
she had a friend over, the girls installed the dolls in an elaborate
classroom in the bedroom, and then stood in the hallway, gabbing,
while the dolls sat alone. Jenna Welch walked by and teased the
girls about why they were talking instead of tending to their students. I thought you were teaching, she said. "This *is* what our
teachers do," Laura said.

Teaching was a conventional and perfectly acceptable choice for
a West Texas girl to make, and Laura never deviated from it. She
entered Southern Methodist University in the fall of 1964—
inexplicably, she said she had been inspired by a biography she read
in ninth grade of an SMU football player—and declared education
as her major. She pledged Kappa Alpha Theta and lived in the

sorority's Georgian brick house, where the girls glided up and down a curving staircase and had their dinner served by houseboys. "When I started at SMU, girls still wore dresses to school the whole time," Laura said. "It was a fairly conservative campus compared with how it was just a few years after that, for the little brothers and sisters of my friends. Even growing up in Midland, they had a different experience than we did. So we weren't wild like that. I mean, people smoked cigarettes—and I did. And they drank beer, and that was sort of the way college kids were wild when I was there."

At Stanford University, Laura's former Lee classmates Mary Ann Ryerson and Tobia Hochman Gunesch were being challenged to think about race and oppression by African-American teaching assistants and fellow students marching for civil rights. At SMU, meanwhile, the campus clung to the culture of the 1950s, with women more intent on acquiring their Mrs. than their B.S. The turmoil of the 1960s that caused widespread campus unrest elsewhere never touched SMU, a rarefied enclave surrounded by parks in an upscale part of Dallas. The waves of trouble in poor parts of Dallas seemed as far away as Newark or Oakland. "It was like a little lapping at the shore," said English professor Marshall Terry, of the social foment of the era.

The photographic record of campus life of that era is seared into memory—the slain students at Kent State; the long-haired innocent tucking the daisy into the rifle of a national guardsman; the angry mob occupying the president's office in Harvard Yard. As President Johnson steadily increased troops in Vietnam amid growing rancorous dissent in 1966, Martin Luther King, Jr., made a historic visit to lily white Southern Methodist University, where he spoke out against the war. While some of Laura's friends remember his visit vividly, Laura Bush, in a rare moment of frankness, said she has no memory of the event. No, campus life at SMU was one of chattering young women lying on their beds, smoking and playing bridge. They obediently kept to their 10 P.M. curfew. No one burned bras.

And Laura would never have done any protesting, said her friend Jan Donnelly O'Neill. Laura shared this almost bizarre disinterest in the nation's tumult with her future husband, who, even at the more politicized Yale, was famously unmoved by the fervent arguments of those he derided as intellectuals. At SMU, Laura studied hard, taught Sunday school, and dated a lot. But she was no grind. "Her room was always the central headquarters for fun. She was never one to tell people, 'I have to study, so everyone has to leave,' " said her Theta sister Susan Nowlin. Lounging on her bed, listening to music, she could even be silly. "One day Laura says, 'I need to practice my Miss America wave.' We all started laughing and asked her what she was talking about. She laughed and said, 'You just never know when it will come in handy.' She put her hand up in the air, middle fingers together and moving it in a mechanical motion. Now when we see her on television before she gets into a car or as she walks to the stage, we'll scream, 'Look! She's doing her Miss America wave!' "

During her sophomore year in college, Laura went back for a weekend to Midland, where she was presented as a debutante. There is a lineup of them—Laura is standing beside her friend Jan, who years later would insist she come over for barbecue with George W. Bush—and they are clutching rose bouquets, their long white gowns shining, their arms fitted into those gloves, up past the elbows.

By the time she graduated from college in 1968, she favored the peasant blouses and bell-bottom pants of hippie girls everywhere, although Laura would never have characterized herself as one. But there were signs that her curriculum and wider reading had pushed her to think beyond her comfort zone. Plenty of her fellow graduates were getting married right away; some had done so in college. That path led from commencement to the altar to the pram. Laura showed no inclination to follow it. She even doubted, albeit briefly, whether she was limiting herself by picking such a traditional career for a woman. Betty Friedan's seminal 1963 work of revolution, *The Feminine Mystique*, and other feminist literature had made an impact even in big-haired, soft-talking, white-gloved Texas, and Laura startled her sweet daddy, who would have done anything for his girl, by accusing him of "programming" her to be a teacher when she could have been a lawyer. It was a rare moment of self-doubt.

Harold Welch was not going to be held liable for limiting his only child's aspirations. "Daddy almost immediately pulled out his wallet," Laura recalled, "and said, 'I'll send you to law school.' He would have loved to."

But, she remembered, "I had to admit, when he did that, that I didn't want to be a lawyer. I wanted to be a teacher."

Before she headed into a classroom, Laura worked on her parents to let her spend the summer in Europe. Jenna and Harold were reluctant to let her go alone; Harold might send his daughter to law school, but he didn't want her bumming around the continent alone, a rucksack on her back. "Originally Laura told us she wanted to go with a group of girls from college on a European camping trip, but we weren't sure about that," said her mother, Jenna. "We were pretty protective." So they agreed she would tour with Harold's brother, Mark, a Dallas surgeon, who had planned a two-week medical conference for himself and his family in several countries. Laura applied for a position with the Dallas public schools, and off she went on what she later laughingly referred to as "the seventeen-day, seventeen-country trip. That's a great way to go to Europe, when you're young. It gives you a real sense of a lot of the countries, and then it gives you the opportunity to know which ones you want to visit for longer times." The constant train and bus travel would stand in stark contrast to her foreign travel thirty years later, when she was swept by military jet and motorcade into the inner sanctums of privilege and power. In her first solo trip overseas as first lady, she seemed bent on re-creating some of that experience—she wanted to browse in the pet shops of Paris that had so charmed her in that early knockabout. She wanted to drag her own daughter Jenna up the steps of that iron marvel, the Eiffel Tower, that she had climbed when she was about that age. Jenna refused to go.

At the end of the summer of 1968, Laura still didn't have a teaching job, so she settled for work in a Dallas insurance office. In a few weeks, though, she was hired to teach third grade, and she moved into an apartment there with three other women from college.

"I walked to that school," she told me. "It was an older neighborhood, and the children there went to private school. They bused in my children from around Parkland Hospital. It was a predominantly African-American school, and it was a really good school. Our principal was very careful to make sure we had twenty students in the class, which was a great small number. But if you have never taught before, twenty was a lot," she said with a laugh. "I loved it. I loved it. My favorite part was the reading. The books were my favorite. After lunch, I would read stories to them, and it was like Charlotte was in our class. And they had a really great time, and I did, too." When she mentioned reading *Charlotte's Web*, I was curious about this woman who so savored literature, but who had learned to carefully guard her emotions in public: Did she cry each time, at the end of the E. B. White classic, when the spider dies? She answered without hesitation, "Oh, sure!" And she seemed to relish the memory.

That first year was a challenge, though, despite the years of play-acting and the education degree. Children in the classroom were not dolls lined up in the bedroom. Laura admits now she was not ready for the rigors of the job. Teacher training is a subject she has returned to again and again, both in Texas and in the White House. Her own experience informed her insistence.

"I don't think I was really prepared to teach," she said to me. There was no formal mentor program, no pairing with veteran educators. "I think you just learn by experience. You just keep trying. I think I'd be a really good teacher now, probably a lot better than I was then. But I also raised two children."

In the official version of Life as Laura that she and her friends tell, there is no mention of yearning as she watched her girlfriends, one by one, settle down and marry. In its place is an almost methodical attention to burnishing an image of Laura as a dedicated career woman, a teacher who saw her work as a calling. But there is this: After just one year in Dallas, she seems to have been lonely, and she decided to move to Houston, where she worked in a downtown office, "which I wanted to, because I was single, and I thought I'd meet people. By January I thought, 'This isn't fun.' I did meet someone, but not at work. I taught fourth grade, then second, and went with them [the second-graders] to third grade." Houston's John F. Kennedy Elementary was a mostly black school in the north part of the city. Blacks were slowly getting some control over their own governance. Johnson's Voting Rights Act had helped swell the voter rolls and step up attendance in the voting booth, and in 1971, for the first time since Reconstruction, a black gained a seat on the city council.

For Laura, the peculiar invisibility that shrouded blacks and Latinos in Midland began to slowly vanish in Houston, and she was increasingly drawn to work in poor schools. "I particularly wanted to teach in a minority school," she said, "and I loved it. I think mainly I just learned about the dignity of every human and every child, and how important every single child is and how important each one of their lives are."

Well, who can disagree with that? It is an aphoristic statement, and certainly right on message. Republican strategists adore Laura's disciplined adherence to the party line of compassionate conservatism. She has the ability to project a sincerity on education that has charmed even her husband's most vociferous opponents, like Democratic Senator Edward Kennedy of Massachusetts. From this hilltop position of advocacy, she has adroitly avoided getting gummed up in the messy ground-level details of funding. But Laura's belief about the importance of every single child is authentic. Her warmth with schoolchildren is real, and making classroom appearances is Laura Bush's single most favorite task. There is never a child who hugs her too tightly. She is not a woman to worry about getting a nose wiped on her silk sleeve. Over and over, I have seen her intuitively drop into a teacher's crouch so she can look right into their faces with those piercing turquoise eyes. This authenticity is what endears her to teachers and librarians all across the country, because in her they find a desperately needed ally, and they cling to that view of her, even as they feel her husband has abdicated his promise to reform education.

Her kids in Houston felt that authenticity. Shy with the teachers, she was really good with the children, said her principal, Vestophia Gunnells. "The kids really did love her," recalls Larry Gatson, a cleaning business owner whom she taught in second grade. "She'd go outside and play with us."

When her second-graders went on to third grade, she went on with them, teaching them for the following year. Laura was happy to hold on to her students, but, in retrospect, worries about whether that model may have failed them.

"I don't think it's a great idea, and lots of schools try it," she said. "The subjects that I was not particularly good at or interested in they were shortchanged in, and the things I like, like reading, they got a double dose in, and they probably didn't end up with great math skills. But it was fun." As she reflected on what she thought had worked in her school year, she focused more and more on her love of reading and the satisfaction she gleaned from infusing her students with a love of books. She decided to enroll in graduate school at the University of Texas in Austin, and get a master's degree in library science.

Privately, her mother despaired. "I remember my mother telling me she had run into Jenna in Midland," recalled a high school acquaintance, "and Jenna sort of wailed to my mother, 'We're worried that Laura is never going to get married. She just ended things with her longtime boyfriend, and now she's going to Austin and getting her master's degree, as a librarian! How will she ever find someone?' "

"Oh, she had plenty of dates," said her friend Pam Nelson, with men who were "mostly very bright. She wouldn't waste her time with anyone who wasn't serious about their future and studies."

In Houston, Laura had moved into the hilariously named Chateaux Dijon, a pretentious apartment complex with turrets, where a young pilot in the Texas Air National Guard named George W. Bush was also living, and drinking, and carousing, and doing Lord knows what to stewardesses, and playing volleyball until late at night in one of the six swimming pools. Their paths never crossed, "thank heavens," Laura once said, with a laugh. At the Chateaux, she explained, she lived on the "sedate" side, and George lived on the "wild side."

She found another guy who lived in the Chateaux Dijon, Jimmy McCarroll, a Houston stockbroker who later went into the oil and gas business, and he became Laura's steady boyfriend for several months. One of Jimmy's best friends was a young lawyer named Joe Longley, who already was married and lived in Austin. Jimmy and Laura liked going to football games, and they would come up to Austin and spend weekends with Joe and his wife, Susan.

The Texas capital in the late 1960s was "Lotusland, full of trees and water, with hippies wandering through the forest," remembers Bud Shrake, a novelist and playwright. "Living was so easy, and laid-back, and half the people were barefoot and topless." One resident fixture was known for dropping acid and climbing into his car with his poodle, and slowly driving all over town with the dog sitting on the dashboard. The hippies and the rednecks mingled and discovered they both liked country music, and Austin gave birth to the Cosmic Cowboy Movement. Willie Nelson arrived in town looking like a car salesman, then grew his hair to his ass. "I saw the parade and threw myself in front of it," he once said of those years. Jerry Jeff Walker and Nelson and Eddie Wilson all played at a joint called the Armadillo World Headquarters, and Longley remembers going there with Laura and Jimmy, or dropping in to a psychedelic rock palace on Congress Avenue. Or they'd all drift over to Eeyore's Birthday in the Park, an annual spring ritual on the banks of Town Lake, where all the groups of people converged to smoke dope and drink kegs and spread peace and love.

"I'm thinking that they were coming up here during the Cambodian invasion," Longley remembers, "and there were peace marches that my wife and I participated in. I don't know if Laura went, but she was pretty sympathetic to that cause."

He found her "wonderful," he said. "She was very warm and highly intelligent and sensitive, very much up on current events." Laura maintains that she was never "political," and she insists she put off meeting her future husband for so long because of his father's political career.

Joe Longley, who is a liberal lawyer, perceives this differently. "Austin is a very political town," he said, "and we all had political discussions. She didn't even strike me as at all conservative. I was really impressed with how sensitive she was to people and issues. She worked in a school that wasn't in the greatest neighborhood, and she really loved it."

Jimmy was much more conservative than Laura was, Longley recalls, and, while he doesn't remember specific political discussions, "she would chime in much more with me than she would with Jimmy. She engaged and made her points well and had them backed up better than we could." Always curious about current literature, Laura initiated a lot of discussions about books. "I liked to read current best-sellers, and she would always have already read everything I thought I was on the cutting edge of. And I am talking about history and Civil War and World War II books and stuff. I guess she saw stuff coming across her desk and just sopped it up."

Armed with her graduate degree in 1972, Laura moved back to Houston and a job as a children's librarian at the McCrane-Kashmere Gardens Library. But she was restless there. She dated steadily but hadn't found anyone who was a perfect match. She missed the elementary school setting, with its opportunity to work with the same children year after year. She was drawn back to Austin, where she had gone to graduate school. Of the cities where she had lived after leaving Midland, Austin's sensibilities suited her best. People seemed open-minded and accepting. It was physically lovely, although hotter than Midland, and verdant, with a wide branch of the Colorado River flowing through the town center. The music and art scene was vibrant; she could have a life of the mind there. And her best friend, Regan, now lived there with her husband, Billy, an insurance agency owner.

So she sought work as a librarian in an elementary school. Again, she purposely chose a poor school, this time in Austin's barrio. In the fall of 1974, she tackled the library shelves at the Mollie Dawson Elementary School. Named for a Texas teacher from the early 1900s, Dawson Elementary School is in southeast Austin, in a neighborhood of ramshackle one-story shingled houses, auto body shops, and carry-out beer joints. There's a storefront church every couple blocks, each with a crude hand-lettered sign, Iglesia. The school's population is 80 percent Hispanic, and 90 percent of its five-hundred-plus students receive free or reduced-price lunches, which is how the federal government measures a school's poverty rate. Among Dawson's other disadvantages is a high transient rate; area landlords raise rents, families have to move, the kids attend yet another new school. Among its advantages is a sense of neighborhood and stability. Most of the students walk to school, which helps parents be more involved, able to attend evening functions and parent-teacher conferences. Its faculty is a tenacious bunch; many of them are twenty- and thirty-year veterans, who now teach the grandchildren of some of their very first students. For years, the Dawson reunions have drawn together existing staff and former and retired administrators. Laura Bush once hosted one at the Governor's Mansion in Austin. "The staff is just extraordinary," said Debbie Shaffer, who became the school's librarian in 1980, a few years after Laura left. "It's a very rewarding place for all of us to be."

Despite its problems, Mollie Dawson has far fewer problems today than it did during Laura's three years there. The population was even poorer, the neighborhood more riddled with crime. "I seemed to have more people in turmoil—refugees of El Salvador, Nicaragua," said Vickie Zelis, a second-grade bilingual teacher for thirty years. The students were socioeconomically deprived and without parental support. Many had parents who were alcoholics or drug addicts, with sisters who took care of them or parents who had to leave them alone when they worked at night. "They were tough, and hard to teach," said Zelis, "and what they got in life was what they got in school."

At Dawson, Laura was part of a teaching team rather than the stereotypical school librarian. In his speeches years later, her husband often would make a joke at her expense. "Laura's idea of giving a speech is to say 'Shhhhhhhh' to a bunch of schoolchildren," he would say with a big grin, and always get appreciative laughter. That joke rankled Laura. She exacted her own revenge by making her own joke that played just as well with her American Library Association sympathizers: "I've been setting the record straight: When I first met George, he was a gregarious businessman whose idea of literature was the sports pages. I'm not saying he never set foot in a library, but until I set him straight, he thought a bibliography was the life story of the guy who wrote the Bible." The text of her speech says, "PAUSE." Then: "I'm kidding, of course." Ahhh-ha-ha—HA! her audience would erupt. But his joke rankled her because it perpetuated the stereotype she hated, of the librarian with the bun and stern expression, frowning as she stood ready to impose fines on overdue books. To Laura, story time was an opportunity to create for her students the same passion for reading that she had. With the primary school students, she used stories to teach the alphabet and phonics. "She would ask them to think: 'What was the character thinking? What is your favorite part? Why? What do you think is going to happen next?' She impressed me as a reading teacher, really, teaching comprehension skills," recalled Vickie Zelis. "It wasn't entertainment, and then you get the kids back in line and send them back to class.

"Some of those kids, they thought books were a foreign object. She had to deal with behavior problems, kids who threw her books down. She was very friendly and very loving but very firm. She had her rules for her library, and you followed them." At Dawson, Laura solidified a belief that she would encourage her husband to adopt as a core value of his presidency: Reading was the new civil right. Without fluency, the future was doomed, for her poor kids who had not a single book in their homes, for kids all across America who could not escape poverty.

She *knew* it, and when she went out for happy hour with her fellow educators from Dawson, over margaritas and salsa and chips, Laura would listen quietly when the rest of them gossiped about their boyfriends. But when she could turn the conversation toward this epiphany she leapt to life. "She just adored her kids, and she was almost fierce in advocating for them," recalled a Dawson teacher who often repaired to the Armadillo World Headquarters with Laura on Fridays. Her speech would quicken, and her sentence structure would grow more complex, in the same pattern she exhibited nearly thirty years later.

Laura carried herself in a professional manner. She didn't much share the ins and outs of her dating life with her work colleagues, but she was not wanting for male companionship.

"She lived in the university area," said Billy Gammon, Regan's husband, "and came to our house once a week to do her laundry. She was a beautiful young woman, and guys were courting her all the time. I never understood why Laura had any free time. If she had any eccentricities it was that she was so clean. She would move into a little dump, and in a matter of weeks, everything would be washed and scrubbed and freshly painted, and she would have planted flowers."

After three years at the school, though, in the very beginning of the 1977 school year, Laura uncharacteristically let on she was starting to date somebody back in West Texas named George Bush. She had taken to going home to Midland on Friday afternoons, making the five-hour drive to visit with her parents and see her friends. "He was rich and a politician and we certainly knew who his father was," said Vickie Zelis. "She had a twinkle in her eye that I'd never seen before. She brought him over to Dawson one day after school, and she said, sort of shyly, 'Well, whoever would like to meet George, well, come on over.'

"And we all said later, 'Oh my *God,* Laura, he's gorgeous!' She was head over heels, and she had her fingers crossed, too."

Even in 1977, achieving that reading fluency that so impassioned Laura seemed impossible for millions of children, generation after generation. It was an enormously daunting process, slowed by conflicting research, crippled by partisan politics, stunted by cuts in funding, complicated most of all by nonreading parents. It would remain a vexing social problem for the next quarter of a century and beyond. It took more than a village. It took more than an impassioned young librarian who could put a book in her lap and read upside down. It took an army of them.

And one of the good ones was about to decommission herself.

CHAPTER THREE

Bush Boy

*We were never mad at each other, because we always had
great opponents.*

—Laura Bush

The man needed a wife.

Not that George W. Bush was exactly a hard-luck case. At thirty-one, he was plenty sexy, with the kind of rakish good looks that could convince a sensible girl to jump into a car beside him and head into the wind. He was quick and witty, and he certainly seemed well educated, what with his Yale and Harvard Business School degrees. His daddy was famous in Texas; his family was rich. But Bush Boy, as his Midland friends called him, had been knocking about for a while. He had done his pilot stint in the Texas Air National Guard, a safe haven during Vietnam for the sons of politically connected Texans. He had spent, by his own admission, "enormous amounts of time and energy courting women," often hosting wild, liquor-sopped affairs at the Chateaux Dijon. He had one broken engagement under his frayed belt, to a Houston woman named Cathryn Wolfman, a pretty and serious student of art and literature. There was a whole collection of dissolute behaviors that Bush refused to catalogue years later, filing them all under one carefully parsed, oft-repeated sentence: "When I was young and irresponsible,

I was young and irresponsible." But episodes included an arrest for drunk driving and an apparent protracted absence without leave from the Texas Air National Guard. Rumors of cocaine use during those years later dogged Bush through his presidential campaign.

By the time Bush Boy's father, George H. W. Bush, was thirty-one, he was a war hero, Yale star, husband, father, and wealthy man. When the peripatetic young George slowed down enough to consider this, he had to recognize that he was "drinking and carousing and fumbling around." Now, back in Midland and trying to make his own money in the oil business, as his father had before him, Bush Boy was renting office space above a soft drink distribution shop. "His office was piled high with soda pop, and he had a desk, and if you wanted to go in there and talk to him, you had to sit on a carton of soda pop," chuckled Robert McCleskey, who had known Bush from their days playing ball in junior high. "Creature comforts—he wasn't into that. Bush Boy was not a big spender. Anytime somebody had an old shirt they were looking to get rid of, Bush Boy would say, 'I'll take it,' " said McCleskey. "He had that old car of his, and it got him from place to place, and that's all he needed." Bush was sleeping in a garage apartment, where the bed-springs were held together with old neckties. He needed a Clorox-the-shelves woman to tidy him up, and fast, because he had decided to run for Congress.

"I didn't think he was really shopping around," said his friend Joe O'Neill. "He was at the age where it was getting awkward to be a bachelor, but I don't think he thought about it." His friends' wives would just shake their heads and smile and put another load of George's wash in their machine. Bush, said O'Neill, "wasn't exactly presidential timber yet. It took some coaching for us to get the girls to go out with him."

O'Neill had married Laura's grade school friend Jan Donnelly in 1972. The couple began finagling to get their friends together when George came back to Midland in 1975, but Laura kept putting them off. She seemed happy enough in Austin, living alone in her house near the University of Texas, working with her kids at Dawson Elementary, enjoying the atmosphere of the counterculture-infused city even if she didn't rush headlong into its freedoms. And she knew the outlines of Bush's life, even if she didn't know him. She knew they both had gone to seventh grade at San Jacinto Junior High, although she couldn't say she had noticed him. He later claimed he always had noticed *her*, but Laura doesn't necessarily believe him, George being a winker and a charmer in just that way. Truth be told, Laura was wary of the Bush family business. "I was so uninterested in politics," she said. "I thought he was someone real political, and I wasn't interested." By politics, she meant not the lofty ideals of it—the chance to transform policy, to serve, to lead. She certainly always voted— Democratic—and had thought her way into strong, left-leaning views. She considered herself a feminist. She worked for more social equity in education. No, when she said she was uninterested in politics, she meant the grubby, manipulative business of it—the pasted-on smile, the constant backslapping and money shaking. The only child in her shied away from the hard-charging competition of it, the very quality that got the Bushes' juices running.

Laura had a sense that she and George were utter opposites, but she also knew why Jan kept bugging her. "Well," she said, with a smile and a shrug, "I guess it was because we were the only two people from that era in Midland who were still single." So she finally gave in, and one evening in the middle of August 1977, home for a visit with her parents, she went over to Joe and Jan's for a backyard barbecue. And there he was. The O'Neills figured George liked Laura right away, because even then he was a man who wanted his sleep so he could get up and run in the morning, and he usually left their place around nine. That evening, he stayed until midnight. He talked nonstop. She seemed to hang on every word. The next night, the two couples went miniature golfing, and then Laura returned to Austin and her workweek.

"She came back and she said, 'Well, I had dinner with George Bush,' " remembers Regan Gammon. "She said, 'He's really a cute guy, and you know, I think he liked me.' " Laura told her mother that George made her laugh. He had a naughtiness she liked.

He found in Laura a thirty-year-old woman who, he wrote in his autobiography, was "gorgeous, good-humored, quick to laugh, down-to-earth and very smart." He might not want them stealing his thunder, or talking over him, but Bush liked his women smart. His mother was intelligent and shrewd; his former fiancée had been quite a reader. He was never afraid of women with opinions; years later, he would select them as his closest advisers and confidants, starting with Karen Hughes, then relying heavily on the brainy Russia scholar Condoleezza Rice. And Laura *was* gorgeous, in a fresh, totally unaffected way. She radiated an easiness of temperament and a self-containment that drew him and seemed to calm his restless, hyperkinetic spirit. He moved immediately to conquest. A few days after the cookout, George flew off to the annual family retreat at the Bushes' compound in Kennebunkport, Maine. After only one day of vacation, he abruptly caught a flight back to Texas. Barbara Bush's antennae quickly went up. He had told her about meeting this "lovely creature," Bar said, and he had been calling Laura repeatedly. Either she wasn't home, or she said she was too busy to talk. Or, worst of all, a man had answered the phone. It was Regan's husband, Billy Gammon, but George had no idea of that. He hightailed it back to Texas to protect his turf. Suddenly, George was driving to Austin nearly every weekend, and Jenna Welch, Laura's mother, started to worry. The bachelor running for the state's 19th Congressional District seemed overeager. She feared her independent daughter would feel hurried along and drop George; Jenna had seen that happen before. "I was afraid George was going to ruin the whole thing because he was rushing it. In the past, when Laura brought home these nice young men from SMU, that had turned her off," she said.

But steady Laura seemed to be holding her breath this time. The courtship raced along. By early October, George was taking Laura to meet the parents. George and Barbara Bush were at home briefly in Houston after a trip to China, where the former congressman had served as ambassador. Soon, big George was heading back to Washington, where he had been director of the Central Intelligence Agency. Young George's brothers were at the house in Houston as well, and ready to torment the new girlfriend they had never met. When the couple walked through the door, Laura looking a bit tentative, Jeb Bush sauntered up to her and exaggeratedly fell to one knee and extended a hand.

"Did you pop the question to her, George, old boy?" Jeb asked. As George turned red, Laura calmly replied for him: "Yes, as a matter of fact he has, and I accepted." That shut the boys up. After a stunned moment, they started to cheer. That was the way George and Bar discovered their eldest was ready to take a bride. "We didn't even know he wanted to get married until he showed up at the door with this beautiful creature, Laura, and announced that she was going to be his wife," Barbara Bush said later. Years before, when he was a Yale student, he had darted into Neiman Marcus on the spur of the moment and emerged with a diamond ring, which he then slipped onto the ring finger of the delighted Cathy Wolfman. This time around, George asked the question without such dramatic flourish. He didn't even have a ring, and Laura didn't get one until years later. "It wasn't a formal thing," recounted Andrew Malcolm, Laura Bush's press secretary during the presidential campaign. "He didn't get down on one knee. Both of them sort of knew by then that marriage would be involved. He just wanted to make it official."

It had been a mere six weeks from George and Laura's first date.

They shocked many of their friends when, six weeks after that, they got married on November 5, 1977, the day after Laura's thirty-first birthday. The O'Neills were stunned at the turn their matchmaking took, considering the differences between George and Laura. "He was definitely not the Clark Gable type—suave, debonair, romantic. He was more the John Wayne type—a polite, take-charge, rugged individual, no-nonsense type of guy who liked to have control of the situation," said Charles Younger, another Bush friend from junior high who had gone away to college and returned to Midland years later to become a successful orthopedic surgeon. "And Laura was more the Marian the Librarian type of girl, not a shrinking violet but certainly quiet and reserved and very ladylike. I think their differences kind of became each other's strengths." Regan Gammon saw George's and Laura's attraction that way as well. "We quickly realized that they were perfect complements to one another," she said. "Laura loved George's energy, and George loved the way she was so calm."

Laura herself refused to gush about her betrothed. Through all the recountings of how they met and wed, she has always refused to describe herself as smitten or head-over-heels. Given her deliberate nature, such uncharacteristic impulsiveness would have struck her as suspect. And such reluctance flows from her sense of modesty and her sense of privacy. Unlike her husband, the extrovert, who frequently says their relationship was "love at first sight," or his mother, who says "George fell madly in love with her," Laura is far more guarded about showing her emotions, believing them privileged information. Her version of the courtship sounds almost pragmatic: "I think it was a whirlwind romance because we were in our early thirties," she said. "I'm sure both of us thought, 'Gosh, we may never get married.' And we both really wanted children." In another accounting, she added, "George was running for Congress and we lived in two different cities. It wasn't like other couples who might let a relationship drag out because they had time to. If we were going to be together, we needed to get married and I needed to move to Midland." (There seems never to have been any suggestion that George might abandon his congressional aspirations in West Texas to join her in Austin.) With both of their roots in Midland, she said, "In a lot of ways I guess I felt like I'd known him all my life without really having known him that well."

Others discerned a giddiness she would not acknowledge. "It was the first time I'd ever seen her sure she was in love," said her friend Anne Lund Stewart. "Oh, she was absolutely crazy about him," said Vickie Zelis, the Dawson colleague who met George when Laura brought him around to the school one Friday. "She was like a lot of women—he was a good-looking, smart guy with a great job, and she was really hoping this was it. They were very attractive people—she never came across as the librarian type with the little bun—and I'm sure there was a lot of sexual attraction between the two of them."

Laura's rapid trip to the altar was certainly the most impetuous thing she had ever done. Having acquiesced to her fiancé's urgent timetable, she then signaled to the Bush clan that she no intention of submerging herself entirely under the mores and traditions of the blueblood family, with its *Mayflower* lineage and its Wall Street wealth. When George took her back to Kennebunkport, and the family, much like the Kennedys at Hyannisport, gathered for one of their incessant athletic contests, his grandmother turned to the quiet Laura and scrutinized her. "And what do you do?" demanded the iron-willed and competitive Dorothy Walker Bush, who in her day had been a fearsome field hockey and tennis player. Laura returned her gaze. "I read, I smoke, and I admire," she told the old woman. "Everybody sat back on their haunches with their mouths on the floor," said Barbara Bush in an interview with the *Washington Post* during the presidential campaign. Laura herself later contradicted her mother-in-law, in a story that appeared in the *New York Times*. "That's totally made up," Laura told the *Times* of Bar's account. "I'm sure I said 'I read.' But I certainly didn't say 'I admire.' " But Barbara Bush reiterated her version of the anecdote to the *Times*, saying that she remembered Laura's three-part answer and her own mother-in-law's reaction. "Mrs. Bush darn near collapsed."

This story and Laura's attempt to modify it are telling. In making clear she would maintain an identity and interests apart from her husband, she established a pattern that she would preserve through each stage of their lives together. Throughout the coming decades, as her bombastic husband moved into increasingly public positions, Laura signaled her independence and steered around any suggestions that she play a role which felt inauthentic to her. But she did not want to be recognized for having done so. There would be no fanfare. She preferred to embrace a form of stealth independence, which allowed her to satisfy herself—her interests and her passions and her energy level—while conforming to traditional expectations of a suitable role for women, and especially the subset of political wives. That way, she could make no mistakes and get full credit for the dignified way in which she comported herself. Over the years, when reporters would attempt to get her to define herself, she would always give a variation on the same theme: "I think I'll be, simply, Laura Bush."

The month of the wedding, Laura's and George's hometown paper, the *Midland Reporter-Telegram,* carried the pictures of the country's most powerful women as chosen by *Harper's Bazaar,* which had heralded the women for having "overcome formidable odds in boldly invading traditionally male-dominated areas."

They were: Katharine Graham, the chief executive officer of the Washington Post Co.; broadcaster Barbara Walters; tennis star Billie Jean King; Lady Bird Johnson, who was called "a spirited and tenacious campaigner for dozens of environmental projects"; Washington state governor Dixie Ray Lee, a biologist who had headed the old Atomic Energy Commission; First Lady Rosalynn Carter; Charlotte Curtis, the editor of the *New York Times* op-ed page; Sarah Caldwell, conductor of the Opera Company of Boston; and

Mary Wells Lawrence, founder of the premier advertising agency Wells, Rich, Greene.

At that moment, no one, and certainly not Laura, could have foreseen that she would wind up on just such a list herself. The contrast between her and the women named could not have been sharper; at that moment she was submitting her letter of resignation as a school librarian, to follow wherever her future husband might lead. In a final bit of irony, Mollie Dawson, for whom Laura's school was named, had also resigned because of a man, but for a wholly different reason. Among the school's archival material was a letter from the early 1900s from teacher Dawson to the superintendent of schools, asking for a raise. Mollie Dawson demanded to be paid the same salary as male teachers and threatened to resign if she were not. The superintendent's reaction was immediate. He accepted her resignation, then promptly turned around and hired a male teacher as her replacement—and paid him more money.

The wedding itself epitomized Laura's talent for forthrightly blending elements of tradition and modernity. While she gave up her job and never worked for pay again, she had no interest in the archetype of the virginal bride, floating down the aisle in a cloud of tulle, her face shielded from her Prince Charming by a veil of lace. Just as he pulled out his wallet and offered to send her to law school, Harold Welch would have happily paid for an extravagant wedding. Laura wanted none of it.

The morning ceremony was small and simple by any measure, and especially considering that the ritual joined together a former debutante and the scion of one of America's most powerful political families. There was no gown. There were no bridesmaids or other attendants. The three other brides on the society pages of the Sunday paper were arranged in brocaded wedding dresses with cascading veils and flowers, complete with elaborate wedding gown descriptions—"candlelight French lace and imported tulle," "molded bodice of lace with short-shirred sleeves and wide picture neckline with scallops," "cascades of lace over bouffant skirt which swept to a chapel train." There is much to be gleaned about social standing and individual intent from the wedding pages all across America. They are a Rosetta Stone of sociology: Which one has the advanced degree? Which one will take her husband's name, and which one will retain her own? Which one wants, at least for that one day, to embrace being the center of attention? In truth, nearly all of them, even the shy ones, want to be fairy princess for a day. But the new Mrs. George Walker Bush wanted none of that. In her antipathy for that kind of regard, Laura Welch was a unique specimen. She always had a certain modesty, if the word means anything anymore. Her wedding day portrait shows a fresh-scrubbed woman with short brunette hair that looked as it did every other day of the week, not an embedded seed pearl in sight. She wore a single strand of pearls, and no other ornamentation except a spray of gardenias, pinned to the waist of the two-piece dress she had bought just days before the wedding, off the rack, in Austin. Described as a "street-length dress of candlight crepe de chine" (a pink-tinged beige, for the lay observer), "styled with a long-sleeved, tucked blouson bodice and pleated skirt," it did little for her figure. There were but seventy-five guests, each set of parents having been permitted to invite only two couples. "We thought we were doing them a favor," Laura said later, "but some of the uncles got their backs up." Those guests had received invitations handwritten by Jenna Welch, since there was no time to send out to the printer. Even the venue reflected Laura's desire for austerity. Instead of using the main sanctuary of First United Methodist Church, the church in which she had been baptized and would later baptize her girls, Laura decided to get married in the chapel.

I sat for a spell in that chapel on my trip to Midland. First United Methodist takes up a whole city block in the vacant and echoing downtown; it's as if the whole town had shrunken away, leaving the church as an island unto itself. With its Spanish blond stucco and its terra-cotta tile roof, the hundred-year-old church remains a steadfast fortress of old Texas. Its slogan, "Sharing Christ from the Heart of Midland," underscored this. Its pastor, C. Lane Boyd, told me that the congregation had searched its collective soul as other congregations moved away and decided to remain downtown. There's an entire parking lot with spaces dedicated only for the disabled on Sundays, testament to an aging population. The sanctuary stays locked during the day, but the chapel remains open for prayer and contemplation, and the day I visited, the late afternoon sun slanted through its stained glass windows, each minimal, each slightly different. It was dim and hushed, serene and handsome and plain, with wrought iron sconces on the walls. I thought how perfect a setting it must have offered, with its muted burgundy seats and practical linoleum floor, how true a mirror of the self-effacing woman I knew only as first lady. Her church was a retreat for reticent Laura over the years, and Reverend Boyd said the congregation always was delighted to see her but tried not to make a fuss.

After the morning nuptials, there was a seated luncheon at the restricted Midland Racquet Club. And according to the announcement in the paper there was a brief vacation in Mexico. But George and Laura's real honeymoon took place the next year, on the baked crust of West Texas, as the newlyweds electioneered in a white Cutlass convertible. For months, as George crisscrossed the district, visiting every local fish fry and pancake breakfast, the couple spent hours together getting to know each other. The candidate would bound onto whatever makeshift stage would have him, speaking of his campaign goals, kissing babies, uttering the same bromides over and over again. His bride stayed by his side, her very presence as a homegrown girl refuting the critics who decried his ambition as suspect Ivy League carpetbagging. If Laura spent those months irritated that she had to share her new husband with the skeptical voters, if she had nagging second thoughts about immersing herself in the business of politics, if there were days when she felt her worst fears about "someone real political" had been realized, she kept those to herself and never let on for years. Only in 1994, once she was first lady of Texas, did she acknowledge: "I worried about the stress of the political campaign combined with the stress of being newlyweds." So he made her a pledge, which became one of the well-worn anecdotes they offered up for public consumption, always to appreciative chuckles. "We had a prenuptial agreement that I would jog with him, and I'd never have to give a political speech," she said. "And, of course, about three months later I found myself on the courthouse steps in Levelland, Texas, giving a political speech, and, of course, I never jogged with him, not even once."

They had both broken their promises, straight out of the blocks. That first speech was squirmingly bad. I've seen her wince and chuckle over it, decades later. Three months into his race, he had a scheduling conflict, and he pressed his shy wife into delivering an address from those courthouse steps in Levelland, a small town in the Texas Panhandle. "And I did it," Laura said. "I started out and I had a great beginning." She tried out the lines about her husband promising her she'd never have to give a speech. "So much for political promises," she said, and she waited for the laughter. "But I hadn't really written a speech, so it sort of dwindled down to nothing," and she mumbled a few things, and sat down. She could not transport the ease she had reading to children, from a book held upside down, to speaking up for a political candidate, even if that man was her husband. It being West Texas, however, "the good thing is, everyone is so nice that every person in the audience, including all the other candidates, were just sort of shaking their heads and smiling at me like I was doing great."

She grasped that the Bushes had a very different family dynamic from the small set of three—mother, father, daughter—so comfortable to her growing up. And she recognized that they were

engaged in a very different sort of business. "It was like Audrey
Hepburn walking into the Animal House," said George's younger
brother, Marvin. "Here was this bright, cerebral, lovely human
being—a very serene-type person—coming into this chaotic envi-
ronment known as the Bush household." She worked hard to figure out their intricacies and to accommodate herself to it. Laura
was not calculating, not in a way that implied manipulation, but
she was serious about her marriage. That was what smart and
really traditional women did: They worked hard to understand
their husbands and adapt. That was Laura's new job. That was
women's work, to do the emotional toting and lifting of the marriage, while the man busied himself out in the greater world. At
one point, as she and George were careening through the towns of
West Texas, Muleshoe and Friona and Littlefield and Bovina, she
sought advice from her mother-in-law, a career political wife with
stints in Congress and the American embassy in Bejing under her
belt, as well as two failed Senate campaigns in Texas. Barbara always had been closely involved in her husband's quests; a Smith
graduate, she was no Mamie Eisenhower content just to turn the
lamb chops. When Laura asked, Bar had a ready answer. "Don't
criticize his speeches," she said. Bar had learned that lesson herself,
by faulting big George on remarks that he had delivered, only to
endure him waving letters in her face for months gushing that his
speech was the best the letter writers ever had heard. Laura faltered. One night, in the Cutlass, ready to pull into the driveway of
the brick ranch house they had purchased on Golf Course Road in
Midland, George asked Laura what she thought of the speech he
had delivered that evening in Lubbock, a few hours away. "Well,
your speech wasn't very good," she began, and he promptly drove
into the garage wall. Laura also told this anecdote again and again.
It became part of a concerted effort to make sure voters, especially
the key group of moderate women, would not interpret her shyness
as subservience. The point of the story was that Laura had strong

opinions and wouldn't hesitate to share them. Implicitly, it also made clear that she wasn't afraid to stand up to her tough mother-in-law, either.

Laura possessed "a great philosophy in life—you can either like it or not, so you might as well like it," Barbara Bush once said approvingly of her daughter-in-law. Over and over, Laura's friends echoed this sense of serenity. "Laura is not a whiner. She is just not a complainer, not ever," said her Midland friend Lynn Munn, who often marveled at her equanimity. "Some people complain just to complain even in a kidding way, and she just doesn't do that."

Despite her stated disinterest in politics, Laura years later revealed some sophistication about the process—and a keen insight into her husband. "George did sort of leap into it," she acknowledged about that maiden run for office, "but even back then he was smart enough to know that a lot of politics was simply timing. You know, there are a lot of would-be governors of Texas sitting around today who never took the opportunity to get into a race when the time was right. If George is good at anything, it's timing." She also indicated that she had raised her concerns with George and plunged onward. Ever adaptable, Laura chose to focus on the positive, and she regarded the months side by side on the road as a great adventure, which gave the two of them time to get to know each other intimately. "We were never mad at each other," she said, "because we always had great opponents."

George Bush lost that race: too green, too smart-assed, too many missteps, the political strategists all said afterward. What he gained, more importantly, was the unshakable loyalty of his new wife. Along that campaign trail, she saw and heard things that horrified and hardened her. Politics looked pretty ugly from her shotgun seat in the Cutlass. Bush's Democratic opponent, a state senator named Kent Hance, hammered away relentlessly at George's pedigree and his outsider status and his holding on for dear life to his daddy's coattails. Hance had spent his life in Texas, gone to public schools in the Panhandle, not preps; attended Texas Tech, not Yale; gone to law school at the University of Texas, where young George had applied but been rejected. Hance knew how to connect with the farmers. He understood instinctively their values and their humor. West Texans were all backslapping, how ya dewin, c'mon over for supper, real friendly, and underneath that, they could be real mean. One day, with Bush sitting right there, Hance started in on a yarn, according to an account in Bill Minutaglio's Bush biography *First Son,* that went like this:

"There was this farmer, sittin' on his fence one day when this big, fancy limousine comes rolling up the dirt road and stops right in front of him. The windows roll down and the fella inside says, 'You know the way to get to Lubbock?'

"The farmer, he chews on the straw for a couple of seconds and points up the dirt road and he says to the chauffeur, 'Go on up the road a couple of miles till ya see the cattle guard, then go left and pretty soon you'll be in town.'

"Well, a while goes by and the farmer sees the big fancy limousine coming back down the dirt road. The window rolls down and the chauffeur says, 'Forgot to ask, what color uniform is that cattle guard wearing?' "

Hance waited for the guffaws and belly laughs to subside, and then, just in case anybody had missed the point, he turned to look at his opponent and said: "You see, that limousine wasn't from around these parts. I think it had one of them Connecticut plates. That where you from, George?"

Laura knew that all George could do was sit and seethe. It got nastier late in the campaign. After a Bush staffer put an ad in the Texas Tech paper for free beer at a "Bush Bash," a Hance staffer sent a mass mailing to some four thousand Church of Christ members, warning those teetotalers that "Mr. Bush used some of his vast sums of money in an attempt, evidently, to persuade young college students to vote for and support him by offering free alcohol to them." Hance weighed in by saying, "Maybe it's a cool thing to do at Harvard or Yale." Bush's aides learned that Hance leased building space he owned to a bar, and urged their candidate to expose Hance's hypocrisy. But George refused. He insisted on taking the higher ground, although one of his strategists was Karl Rove, a cherub-faced former college Republican known for hardball tactics, who already had been accused of possible dirty tricks in the Watergate era. At a press conference, Bush settled for fuming that Hance's campaign "had been funny. First he attacked my family, then my background, and now my morals."

Watching such tactics in her quiet way, Laura felt a spark of anger. These were the very qualities she loved and admired in George: his family, his background, his morals. He was a good and decent man. She knew it, she felt it, she basked in it. The idea that he was some snotty rich kid from back East! Had she gotten married at the compound in Kennebunkport, as his parents had? Did she have some society wedding? Did she even have a diamond? No! They lived modestly. Over time, she would learn to close her ears when George's opponents attacked him, but she would never get used to it. Here was a woman who had voted solidly Democratic, who had spoken up against the bombing of Cambodia, who had called herself a feminist, who had championed the future of poor minority children, now campaigning with a man who opposed the Equal Rights Amendment, sanctions against South Africa, and Andrew Young's appointment as United Nations ambassador. She refused to think about all of that. She was unable to assess his political stands objectively, to regard him with the cool intellectual analysis she might bring to bear on others she observed. That ended right there, in that first political campaign. For

God's sake, he was her *husband,* not her candidate, or her governor, or her president.

Seeing George or any of the other Bushes assailed was one of the
few scenes that could rouse Laura from her sometimes preternatural calm. She can move almost languidly, and she is capable of sitting attentively stiller than anyone I have ever seen, while her
husband fidgets in the seat beside her. You have to study her to
know when she is displeased, the expression is that subtle. The face
stays composed just as it was a moment before, but the muscles outside the corners of the mouth tighten, and her lower lip purses ever
so slightly. Certainly her girls and her husband have come to know
That Look. But when the Bushes are under attack—and Laura can
put seemingly dispassionate and reasonable criticisms into this
category—her dissatisfaction animates her entire body. *Texas
Monthly* writer Paul Burka, a longtime political observer, caught
this during an interview in the Governor's Mansion in Austin, when
he and Laura were making political chitchat and the antics of a
prominent Texan popped up. "I observed that he had once accused
the Republicans of a nefarious plot to embarrass his family. Suddenly Mrs. Bush leaned forward in her chair. 'Not the Republicans,'
she said. 'Us! The Bushes!' It wasn't just her words that made the
moment embed itself in my memory, but the force with which she
delivered them and her body language, which conveyed solidarity
with her husband across the room. That brief exchange provided a
rare glimpse into the private world of the Bush clan; its power and
intensity, its unity and sense of loyalty, flashed before our eyes."

Burka observes that Laura can be divided into two sides. "You
could call one side Laura and the other side Bush," he wrote. "Laura
remains a woman who is down-to-earth, without affectation or
pretension—someone who, as she once said, would be just as happy
puttering around in her garden as being first lady. Her reluctant

attitude toward public appearances hasn't changed much. . . . But the other side of her is that she is totally a Bush. Not all of her education has come from reading the succession of books that the former teacher and librarian keeps stacked on her bedside table and on the floor beneath it. Being a member of the clan has also been a central part of the education of Laura Bush: She has learned what is expected of her, and she will do what she has to do." And part of what is expected for admittance into the Bush inner circle, said biographer Minutaglio, is a personal sublimation. "She understands the requirements: 'My role is to let go and submerge my own ambitions in some way in service to this family.' . . . It's for the greater good."

After George lost the race in November of 1978, he and Laura settled into a routine identical to that of the other oilmen and their wives. George went downtown to his office in the Petroleum Building and hoped his wells would quit coming up dry. Laura cooked and cleaned and gardened and read. She got involved with the Junior League. Weekends, they socialized with other couples, Bill and Lynn Munn, Jan and Joe O'Neill, Don and Susie Evans, Ann and Clay Johnson. They all rode the ups and downs of the capricious oil business. Sometimes they were flush, and sometimes they were scuffling. They had barbecues at each other's houses or dinner at the country club, and Sunday mornings, they went to church. Behind that pleasant rhythm, the political education of Laura Bush was continuing. Within months, her father-in-law was running for president and frequently calling to consult with his son. George was raising money for him in West Texas, sometimes making fifty phone calls a day. Ronald Reagan eventually became the Republican Party's nominee in 1980, and then at the convention, Reagan asked big George to become his running mate. A little more than three years after her wedding and her second campaign, Laura watched as her father-in-law was sworn in as vice president of the United States. The seeds of her perseverance as a political wife, and her ability to divide her persona into public and private realms, were firmly established and growing. The loyalty was in place, ready to deepen when big George later would run for president and be subjected to criticism she found baseless and cynical.

Another pattern of political partnership was developing. Although George immediately had broken his promise that Laura would never have to give a political speech, overall, he would not ask his wife to go beyond her personal comfort in service to his political aspirations. He himself did not venture beyond his comfort zone. Being a Bush meant living in a proscribed world. One ate certain foods and wore certain clothes. One vacationed in a certain spot, and fraternized with certain people. To George, who had had an uneasy relationship with his fellow students at Andover, Yale, and Harvard, those individuals who chanced something, or pushed themselves, were suspect. They were sneeringly dismissed as strivers. So George would never ask Laura to become something other than what she was. Being true to oneself was a proud Bush quality, and they defined that as staying the same. This is the very trait that makes people say of both George and Laura that they are "comfortable in their own skin." In this way, they were perfectly suited to each other. People respond to that comfortability; voters clearly like it. They find in it a sincerity and stability that is reassuring, even more so in troubled times. But it is a trait that also is self-limiting because if reaching for something is not in one's nature, then it follows that intellectual exploration can be seen as a personal betrayal. (It was no coincidence that George Bush derided David Gregory, the NBC correspondent, when, in Paris, Gregory posed his question to French president Jacques Chirac in French. Bush is the sort of person who thinks an American trying out another language is a pretentious ass.) For Laura, life with George meant that the circumstances of their life might force her to adapt to something she would not have chosen. But he would never directly request that she change anything about herself. George put it on the record: She could do whatever she wanted to do. Including nothing.

From the beginning, George appreciated that she was sure about who she was. He came quickly to rely on her calm and her remarkable emotional clarity. She remained true to herself, and he respected that. When she lived in Midland, she wore white shirts and jeans. When they moved to Dallas after George took control of the Texas Rangers baseball team and Laura began to move in the big-haired, big-moneyed set of Texas matrons, she wore white shirts and jeans. In interview after interview, her oldest friends uttered the same thing: "What you see with Laura is what you get." Regan Gammon groped to be more descriptive. "She's just . . . I don't know how else to put it . . . real." Their unanimity on the topic was perfect for the message discipline of Bush-Cheney 2000 and later in the White House, but its very usefulness did not make it any less true. Of all the parts of politics that irritated Laura, the cynicism about politicians and surrogates and their motives drove her maddest of all. She had held being true to herself as her dearest principle of political wifehood, and it infuriated her no end that her smallest habits were overanalyzed and deemed an elaborate orchestration, most probably by that clever molder of all things, Karl Rove.

Sitting with her in the living room of the family quarters of the White House several weeks after the January inauguration, I reminded her of The Kiss. At the close of the Democratic convention the previous summer, Al Gore had grabbed Tipper and given her a passionate kiss, so fervent that her head arched back and her blond hair tumbled free. The photo was remarkable, and it was carried in thousands of news outlets, and the act itself was dissected and analyzed by pundits for days. How would it play? Would it earn him the respect or the ridicule of the swing female voters? Some columnists wrote of being utterly revulsed. I suggested to Laura the possibility that The Kiss had been spontaneous, and that when I had posited this to a colleague, I was dismissed as hopelessly naive. Laura broke in with a sardonic laugh. "Oh, that, that was real?" and then she feigned being dumbstruck at the idea. "Well, I think you're really right," she said. "I don't think there are that many political people who are so calculating. I think that's some of the cynicism. Somehow, the press and the public, or maybe it's only the press," and here she laughed again, and gave me a mock reproving glance, "thinks that every single move is calculated. And that's just not the case, for a lot of political figures I know, and for most people."

The longer they were married, George found that he could not function without this "realness" and calm. Laura always demurred. Even for what she considered her most important responsibility— being his wife—she refused to take any credit. "He acts like I steady him, but the fact of the matter is, he steadies me," she said.

When I asked their friends in Midland what he saw in her back in 1977, they all recited versions on this theme: She had settled Bush Boy down, in her mild way. His parents thought she was the perfect wife. "She's special," said her father-in-law, the former president. "She's a very wonderful wife for George. I mean, golly, she can calm him down." George thought she was the perfect wife. "I have the best wife for the line of work that I'm in," the president once said. "She doesn't try to steal the limelight."

When I asked what Laura saw in George, the answers didn't come as quickly. Robert McCleskey leaned back in his chair, looked at me a good long moment, and grinned. Mounted and stuffed heads of antelope, water buffalo, and gazelles, trophies from his frequent African safaris, gazed down on us. Then McCleskey sat up and reached into a desk drawer. He rooted around for a minute and withdrew a yellowing snapshot. Without a word, he pushed it over to me. It was a photo of George, circa 1977, in a dusty oil field, squinting under the hot Texas sun. He was wearing a hideous orange and mustard-yellow pop-art-patterned shirt, and his bare arms were brown and muscled. He had longish hair, curly, and that dead-on-gaze, filled with mirth, and that sexy sly smile. "Well then," I said. "I see." And McCleskey chuckled.

But what Laura really saw in George, besides his crackling

chemistry, besides the five funs in one description, was his need. She knew with assurance that he needed her. And she wanted to be needed. Being needed did not feel like surrender to Laura Bush. It was not confining or suffocating. Being needed felt purposeful and satisfying because her husband's happiness and success were possibly more important than her own. In the years to come, when they made decisions about their life together, she would assess the potential change from exactly that perspective: Would it make George feel happy and successful? And after they had determined, together, that it would, off she would go again with him, ever adaptable. Whatever changes came to them, and they would face colossal, even tragic ones, she had constancy in her marriage: He needed her.

CHAPTER FOUR

Motherhood and Baseball

When Barbara and Jenna were babies, I'd still have a few hours of light after they went to bed. One night I was in the garden, the babies were asleep, safe in their beds, and I remember thinking, "This is the life."
—Laura Bush, in 2001, in *Texas Monthly*

Laura Bush rarely shares her reflections. So when she said, "this is the life," there is an ache to it. We didn't know her then, and we know her now, and we grasp that her life now is not that sweet and satisfied idyll; it is watching soldiers wounded in Iraq try to salute and hearing poor child after poor child struggle to read in bad school after bad school and having tourists tramp through her house. The babies are in college, sometimes vexing her to the core. Hers is a public life, with its own rewards and extraordinary perquisites. But her memory of that moment is a piece of simple poetry, a celebration of a woman who at thirty-five had been made complete. She was absolutely right, as Laura usually is, about herself. She has given birth to the children she so fervently wanted. She has replaced in the cycle of humanity the young life she snuffed out. The early death of Mike Douglas at seventeen has made her all too aware of the fragility of life, but at the moment of this recollection, her babies are asleep, cherub mouths breathing softly, and she is satisfied that she has made them safe, and now she can be alone, in her garden at twilight, reveling in the rightness of her world. For this moment, George, with his bombastic personality and easily read emotions, is somewhere offstage.

Laura would hate her life rendered as a literary theme, despite her love of literature. She would hate this public dissection. She's a private woman who shuns such analysis. But she is a first lady, ours, her public, and we wonder about her, and how she has managed to compose a life for herself out of the discontinuity that her husband's ambitions imposed upon her. It is too pat to declaim, "Oh, she knew what she was getting into all along." Who among us does, really? Life is not that kind of linear journey for most people, and especially not for most women, with a starting gun and a finish line off in the distance, with an identified goal that can be attained if only we persevere and jump over the hurdles in our path. And it certainly has not been that for Laura Bush.

They were beautiful babies, Barbara and Jenna, named for each of the grandmothers. From the outset, they outfoxed their parents. The girls had switched it up in the womb, Barbara born with the personality of Laura and her mother, Jenna, and Jenna just like George and his mother, Bar. They entered their parents' lives after George and Laura had nearly given up hope of having their own children. The couple had been trying to conceive for a few years without success, and finally, they resigned themselves to visiting the Gladney home in Fort Worth, where Laura's parents had gone a generation before to seek a second child after Jenna Welch's repeated miscarriages. Many of George's and Laura's friends already had adopted children from Gladney, and the Bushes' application there was pending. They were awaiting a home visit from the caseworker when Laura's doctor called them with good news: She was pregnant. A subsequent sonogram revealed she was carrying twins. George H. W. Bush was vice president of the United States, and now his eldest son was going to be a father.

"We were thrilled," Laura said. "We had waited a long time to have children and so when we got to have two at once, we were especially thrilled." George continued going downtown to his office in Midland, where his oil company, Arbusto, kept drilling over and over, sometimes hitting oil and sometimes not. Laura read her baby books and grew ever larger inside her five-foot-two frame. "Oh, she was huge, plodding along," her friend Lynn Munn recalled. Laura did not feel all that confident about her pregnancy. In the fall of 1981, as her feet and ankles swelled, her doctor grew concerned, and Laura said she avoided the baby aisle when she went grocery shopping. Acutely aware of her mother's history and her own age, and her difficulty getting pregnant, she was afraid to hope. Finally, she was confined to bed. It wasn't so bad because Laura always had been one of the great champions of sedate living, able to lie on the sofa and read and sip soda for hours on end. Then she developed toxemia, a grave condition in which blood pressure rises and the mother's arteries constrict, decreasing the blood flow to the placenta and diminishing the nutrition available to the babies. Suddenly, her babies were at risk, and so was she.

George was alarmed. He would say later that the imperiled pregnancy was the biggest challenge they faced together. Seven weeks before her due date, Laura was rushed from Midland to Baylor Hospital in Dallas, where her uncle practiced and where the neonatal unit had sophisticated equipment. Toxemia is a complication full of anguish, because each day that the babies remain in utero receiving the nourishment so vital to their health, the mother loses a little more of her own hold on life. Monitoring that balance is fraught with desperation, as doctors and parents weigh how long to let a mother nurture her unborn child at grave cost to herself. Finally, the doctors made a decision: They wanted to take the babies, no matter how premature they were. They might be too small to survive outside the womb. George, terrified he might lose his wife, agreed. Laura refused. "These babies are going to be born healthy," she said. "They will stay with me until they're big enough." He bowed to her will. "She wanted to give our babies the best possible chance for survival," George said. "She was heroic. There was unbelievable will to protect our children. I remember to this day how confident I became because of her. She's a determined woman."

That fall, George was continuing to build a profile for himself by chairing the local United Way campaign, and so he was unable to stay with Laura in Dallas for long periods of time. He drove back and forth a few times a week, a distance of nearly 350 miles, and right before Thanksgiving, he returned home. Laura's doctor called on the morning of November 20.

"You're having your babies tomorrow," she said. He was worried, and worried about how Laura would take this news.

"Are you sure?" George asked. "It's five weeks early."

"Well, unless you want your wife's kidneys to fail . . ." the doctor said, and that was enough.

The next morning, he was there when the girls were delivered by cesarean section. "I was in the operating room and I can remember showing them to Laura," George said. "And I'm an emotional person. I got weepy. And then I realized that our life had changed forever in a positive way, that these little human beings were little women that just needed a daddy and a mom to love them. She loves our daughters more than anything, would lay her life down for them. And nearly did at birth." In her usual way of deflecting his praise, and preventing his words from defining her in more emotional terms, Laura said, "But they were big. They were 5-4 and 4-12 for five-week premature twins. And they were in great shape and we were very, very relieved." The agonizing pregnancy and delivery laid a foundation for the way she would regard her girls all her life: "We never took our children for granted. Ever."

According to her friends and her mother, Laura brought the same calm and patience to mothering twins that she did to every other aspect of life. "They weren't bad babies, and she had help—she got a maid—to help her in the daytime," said Lynn Munn. "I don't remember that being a particularly frantic time. They were just so thrilled to have those babies."

Laura was exceptionally fortunate to have her own mother just a few blocks away, and she and the babies saw Jenna and Harold almost daily. The babies' other grandparents were across the country, now installed in the vice president's residence, a white Georgian home on the grounds of the U.S. Naval Observatory. "My husband was so delighted to have grandchildren," Jenna Welch remembered, "and I know Laura has told so many people about his late morning visits. Poor Laura would get them down for their naps at about 11:00 A.M., just get them settled down and asleep, and Harold would come over and open the front door and call out, 'Are the girls awake?' And, of course, they were then."

As they grew into toddlers, and Jenna organized their various mischiefs, a pattern they would continue as teenagers, George often grew exasperated. Laura never raised her voice. "She was just the type that didn't bat an eye," said Munn. "You know, tells them not to do it, but she doesn't let it get to her." She read to them every day, and crooned to them. Their father sang them Yale fight songs, and one can only speculate how that might have solidified their rambunctious natures. From those early years, Laura was reluctant to enforce limits on the girls, because she so enjoyed their high spirits. She herself had been such a good child that she had little personal experience in handling sibling rivalry or the usual testing of parental authority, and often she would default to a philosophical "kids will be kids" attitude. She was a doter, with a tendency toward being permissive. Years later, in a speech during the presidential campaign, she noted wryly, "Babies don't come with sets of instructions. Before George and I were married, we had a couple of theories on raising kids. Now we've got a couple of kids and no theories."

During those Midland years, when Laura went into the garden at dusk to relax, she was not just seeking respite from the exhausting work of motherhood. She had some problems with her husband, too. There he was, a married father, the eldest son of the vice president of the United States, and he was failing at the oil business and hitting the booze too hard. His frugality often crossed over into a crass cheapness. Folks around Midland had a hard time buying George's act on money. The way they saw it, his family was rich, his father was second in line to lead the most powerful nation in the world, and George didn't have money to pick up a round of drinks? Every now and then Laura would catch him doing things that flat-out embarrassed her. One year, he collected all the Christmas cards he had received at the office from various oil suppliers, crossed out the printed names, and wrote "Merry Christmas from George and Laura," then mailed them to their friends. When I heard this, I was sure it had to be George's idea of a joke. And another version of the story had George's friends pulling this prank, because it was just so believable he'd do such a thing. "We saw them at a cocktail party," said one of those who got the cards, "and we started kidding him— 'Hey, you got a second list of poor friends aren't good enough to get the regular Christmas cards?' And George says, 'There's nothing wrong with those cards! Those are perfectly good cards!' And Laura was standing right there and she got mad. She said tersely, 'That is going too far.' "

By January of 1986, Bush's business began to go from shaky to disastrous. The price of oil plummeted from a high of $37 a barrel a few years before to a low of $9 by the time of George's fortieth birthday in July. The boom had started in 1978, the year George was running for Congress, and people started projecting oil would hit $100 a barrel. The town entered what Jan O'Neill called its "doodah days." The thought of liquid gold made a lot of folks crazy. Let's buy a yacht; we'll worry about where to find water later! Let's buy a jet; we can always build a bigger airstrip! Women showed up with rings so huge they nearly needed a crane to hoist their hand. Town officials green-lighted construction of three forty-foot office towers—skyscrapers! In Midland! Rolls-Royces began gliding down Wall Street and idling outside the Racquet Club. It all lasted less than a decade, and when oil busted, it busted in as spectacular a fashion as it had boomed. Six banks went under, as well as dozens of the support businesses like real estate, oil services, and downtown retail. Independent oilmen like Bush were going under every day, and it looked as if his company was headed that way, unless he could sell out.

"Everybody was in pretty much the same boat," said Susie Evans, the wife of Don Evans, who became Bush's commerce secretary. "And everybody pulled together. When times were hard, we had dinner parties." At those parties, George drank too much. Laura would tell him he should quit, "usually the next morning," she said. Although George himself has readily acknowledged that drinking interfered with his life, the couple's friends always have been reluctant to flatly state he was a drunk. "He wasn't a severe alcoholic who really had to struggle to come to terms with it and work on it," said Lynn Munn. "I think so much more has been made of it. 'Wild' in Midland isn't like 'wild' somewhere else. We are talking about sitting at the Racquet Club and having one too many, where the men act stupid and the wives are rolling their eyes." George never drank during the day, and he didn't drink every night. But "once he got started, he couldn't shut it off," said Don Evans. "He didn't have the discipline." There had been no more drunken-driving episodes: In fact, the daughter of Jim McAninch often baby-sat for the twins, and "George would drive her home late at night, after his social events," McAninch said. "I never saw him drunk. If I had, I wouldn't have let him drive my girl." But there had been a few incidents over the years when Bush lost control of himself and behaved like a jackass.

One afternoon, on business in Dallas, Bush went for lunch to a Mexican restaurant, where he saw Al Hunt, the *Wall Street Journal*'s bureau chief, and his wife, Judy Woodruff, and their four-year-old son. It was early April in 1986, and *Washingtonian* magazine had asked a series of inside-the-Beltway pundits to predict which candidates they thought would be on the presidential ballot in 1988. Hunt's entry was "Kemp and Indiana Senator Richard Lugar against Hart and Robb." That was all it said—one line.

George strode over to Hunt and Woodruff's table, according to Minutaglio in *First Son*. "You no good fucking sonofabitch, I will never fucking forget what you wrote!" Hunt heard the vice president's son holler. As Bush raged about the *Washingtonian* article, the newsman stared at him. So did Hunt's wife and their little boy. Hunt knew he hadn't attacked the vice president in any way; he couldn't figure out what had caused Bush's explosion. "He was clearly quite lubricated," Hunt said, and he remembered thinking: "This is a guy who's got problems."

Laura knew that. She was not among those who saw his problem as not particularly serious. Sometimes, she was there when George got into his cups, and she characterized him as thinking he was funnier than he was. "And isn't that what every drunk thinks?" she thought to herself. Sometimes, she was home alone at night, putting the girls to bed herself, while the business drinks he was going to have stretched into drinks with dinner, and Benedictine and brandy afterward. She was the one who woke up with him all those mornings when he had a hangover. Initially, she talked to him about cutting back. When they were out, she might give a nudge that no one else saw, to signal him not to order another round. Frequently, he ignored her. Eventually, she began imploring him to quit entirely. Finally, she delivered her famous ultimatum: "Me or Jim Beam," to hear him tell it. He was almost forty years old, and she wanted him to grow up, gain some confidence, and shake the sense that he always would be in his father's shadow.

To celebrate his birthday, the Bushes planned a weekend getaway at the Broadmoor Hotel in Colorado Springs in late July of 1986. They went with Don and Susie Evans; Jan and Joe O'Neill,

the couple who had introduced them; Penny Royall, a recently separated friend; and Bush's brother Neil. Dinner that Saturday night
was extravagant, with many toasts made with $60 bottles of Silver
Oak cabernet. Bush woke up as usual for his ritual morning run,
but he felt pretty rotten doing it. The other members of the party
were hung over as well, and more than one of them made the familiar "never again" promise. Bush was the one who quit drinking,
completely, without any fanfare. "I don't remember any announcement," Laura said. "I actually remember it more at home than at the
Broadmoor. We joked later about it, saying he got the bar bill and
that's why he quit. There were a lot of jokes that I said it was either
me or Jack Daniel's. I didn't really say that. I think George said that.
He made it into the funny story."

The way she saw it, she hadn't made him do anything; she had
pushed him to embrace quitting for himself, not for her and the
girls. But his reflections on his drinking days indicated he finally
had grasped the extent of his problem and its impact on his family.
"I realized that alcohol was beginning to crowd out my energies and
could crowd, eventually, my affections for other people. When
you're drinking, it can be an incredibly selfish act," he said.

Laura said firmly, "The person who stopped drinking was George.
He had been working toward it for a long time. I think for a year
at least he'd been thinking, 'I really need to slow down or quit.'
Most people who try to quit drinking first think, 'Well, I'm just
going to only have one drink.' And I think in his mind he thought,
'Well, that's what I'll do.' And then, of course, it didn't really
work. Like for everybody, just about, who tries, it doesn't really
work."

But she had been the impetus. There were two reasons that
Laura Bush was the individual most responsible for making George
W. Bush the president of the United States. That was the first. If he
hadn't stopped drinking, he never would have achieved that. "He
was very disciplined in a lot of ways except for the drinking," she

said, "and I think when he was able to stop drinking, that gave him a lot of confidence and made him feel better about himself."

There, she had done it again: Laura neatly had diverted any sense of personal accomplishment in her marriage back onto her husband. She knew that building confidence in him meant he would need to take credit for his own achievements, personal, financial, and political, rather than feeling his wife was somehow managing him behind the scenes. And she didn't want the credit, anyway. What gave her satisfaction was seeing him grow. In his generous way, he praised her. "She is just a very calm and loving person who reminded me in a mature and sobering way that going to a party and deciding to, you know, I'd be on four bourbons on the rocks, which is not all that smart," said George.

She had another reason for excising the "I thought this" and "I wanted that" from her discussions of George's drinking or any other aspect of their lives. To Laura, such elaboration on personal hopes and problems in the media or even among acquaintances offended her sense of privacy and reticence. She might see the necessity of it, and its usefulness in humanizing her and her husband as candidates and later leaders, but it pained her. The much touted "realness" of Laura does not extend to splaying human frailties and skirmishes about, especially for public entertainment, like some weepy fool on confessional daytime TV. It wasn't that she lived in denial, she just kept all discontent and apprehension behind a curtain tightly drawn against even close friends. Her longtime friend Nancy Weiss, who was so close to the couple that she introduced George Bush at the 2000 Republican National Convention, was shocked when she learned during the campaign about the fatal car crash in Laura's senior year of high school. Laura had never mentioned it to her in the more than twenty years they had been friends. "It was such an acute and painful thing in her young life," said Weiss, that "once she got over the grief, she put it away, and now she just won't go there."

Another example of Laura's shield came during an extensive

interview that NBC's Tim Russert conducted during the campaign with both Bushes. At one point, Russert tried to elicit from them a sense of how difficulties might have shaped them. He started by asking George, "What was the worst thing that ever happened to you?"

"I don't know," George began. "I guess the worst thing was watching the economy collapse around me in Midland, in the mid-1980s, and wondering what's going to happen not only to my investors, but to the people that I was working with. And it's hard to describe what it's like to be an economy business and see the price of the commodity just collapse . . . when the price of oil went from $18 to $10 in a couple of months. And I was a small, independent oil explorationist. We had probably, I can't remember, twelve or thirteen employees, all of whom were dependent upon our ability to survive and have cash flow. . . . And it was very worrisome, not only for me and Laura but for the people with whom I was working."

And then Russert turned to Laura, who had been able to take a few minutes while her husband answered to prepare her own response.

"Have you ever known adversity, Mrs. Bush?" Russert asked.

"I think I've been very blessed," she answered. "I was lucky to have parents who were great parents, who really liked children. Sure, there have been tragedies, you know, in both of our lives, but in general, I think we've been very blessed." And that was that. Russert did not follow up to ask her about what those tragedies might have been, and Laura did not offer. She had subtly moved the conversation away from any probing for tribulation, and her husband immediately picked up on the change.

"Yeah, we have" been very blessed, he agreed. "That gives us kind of a political question. 'What adversity have you gone through to make you more compassionate?' . . . I'd like to answer it this way. You know, what positive things in your life have made you be a more loving person? I mean, what is it that allows you the confidence to run for president? . . . And I believe it's how we were raised. We were incredibly fortunate."

When he talked about how he turned his life around at forty and quit drinking, George Bush also gave the credit to the Lord. The summer before, he had engaged in a long conversation at the family's annual Kennebunkport vacation with an old family friend, the Reverend Billy Graham. Since then, he had been on a spiritual quest to deepen his faith. He had been part of a men's Bible study group at First United Methodist Church, and began reading what he usually called the good book cover to cover. Eventually, he gave his life over to God's will, and began sprinkling his conversation with references to Jesus Christ. There were those who thought they saw the hand of Laura in this conversion as well. George had been a lifelong Episcopalian until joining Laura's church after their marriage. But George embarked on his journey into evangelical Christianity without insisting she accompany him. Laura's faith is of a different and more traditional variety, more liberal in its interpretation of theology than his, more compassionate on social justice than is comfortable for most on the religious right. It is less emotional, less overt, more private.

In Midland, a predominantly conservative and Republican town, Laura's church, First United Methodist, boasts a fairly diverse congregation in terms of conservatives and liberals, says its pastor, C. Lane Boyd. There have been spats among parishioners, including a serious one over abortion. When the dust settled, however, the brochure rack outside the sanctuary doors made it clear where the church stood: The pamphlet outlining United Methodist's social justice positions states that "homosexual persons are individuals of sacred worth," that "tragic conflicts of life with life . . . may justify abortion, and in such cases we support the legal option of abortion," and that people have "a duty to consider the impact on the total world community of their decision regarding childbearing and should have access to information and appropriate means to limit their fertility, including voluntary sterilization." Much like Laura herself, Boyd tries to keep equanimity in his church by appearing impartial and keeping his political opinions to himself. "I don't use the pulpit for that. Church is a sanctuary from community conflict," he said, even though his congregants are lively debaters. "There are times that we have to take a moral stand. We failed. We have horse racing. I have some opinions, but I haven't shared them from the pulpit."

George did not impose any of his new lifestyle choices on his wife. He did not ask her to give up drinking or smoking or to practice a more charismatic faith. And she didn't do any of that of her own volition, either. She likes a margarita or two with her Tex-Mex food, and a glass of white or red wine at cocktail hour and with dinner. At some point, she gave up smoking in public, although even now she has a cigarette when she is among friendly troops, those with unquestionable loyalty. Unlike many reformed drinkers or smokers, with their annoying habits of loudly proclaiming how ill cigarette smoke made them, or how destructive a vice alcohol could be, George Bush never put down imbibers. In Alexandra Pelosi's *Journeys with George,* a documentary about the 2000 presidential campaign, the candidate calls NBC producer Pelosi to the front of his plane. Some of the traveling cameramen have rigged up a blender on the campaign plane, so they can enjoy regular nightly margaritas at the end of their day. The whirring and grinding of the ice and the party music has gotten to be too much for Pelosi, the daughter of California Democratic congresswoman Nancy Pelosi, and she is at war with the cameramen. The candidate attempts to broker a peace, but it's clear he's on the side of the margarita makers.

"Look, these guys are just up there trying to have a good solid margarita. . . . You know it's innocent fun, and you stepped in, and like, you rained on their parade," Bush scolds Pelosi. She tries another tack, asking him, "What's it like to be in the front of the plane with all these animals?"

"These are my people!" he says. "It takes an animal to know an animal! I like the animals!"

In his one-on-one relationships, George Bush was not the sort of conservative to impose his will on anybody else. He saved that for public policy.

While George celebrated his fortieth birthday wining and dining in comfort with friends at a luxurious hotel, Laura chose to mark hers exploring in the wild. She went rafting down the Grand Canyon with Regan Gammon, Peggy Weiss, Marge Petty, and Jane Ann Fontenot. It was a week away from husbands and children, from the teeth that needed brushing and the meals that needed cooking and the errands that needed running, from the business woes besetting Midland and bedeviling the husbands. Every mother knows *that* list by heart. It was a providential spell of rejuvenation, because the Bushes were about to be hurled into a whole new arena of life.

After the price of oil bottomed out in 1986, George developed what he later called a "bail-out strategy." It basically involved luring a bigger company to buy him out, so that his investors might stand a shot of getting their money back. A few months after his fortieth birthday, the Harken Energy Corp. came along with a sweetheart deal: George would get stock worth $320,000 in exchange for his stake in his oil company, and also pull down $80,000 a year as a consultant. The terrible worry he had about leaving his employees in the lurch was assuaged when Harken hired several of them, and Bush worked his friends to get jobs for the rest. What Harken got from the deal was an association with the son of the vice president. "His name was George Bush. That was worth the money they paid him," said Harken founder Phil Kendrick, who had stayed on as a consultant after selling the company a few years before.

With money in his pocket, his employees taken care of, and no daily obligations, George turned his attention toward his father's campaign for president. He wanted back in the game he had deserted after his failed congressional bid in 1977. And he wanted to be on the ground in Washington, where he could keep an eye on his father's campaign operatives. Loyalty was Job One in the Bush family business, and young George intended to enforce it. The Bushes found a townhouse on Massachusetts Avenue, not far from the vice president's residence and the stately embassies that lined the major thoroughfare. The family moved in during the summer of 1987. The girls were five, and Laura went on ahead, with Lynn Munn, to set up the house. The move apparently went seamlessly. Laura had an unusual, almost intimidating ability to take an empty house loaded with hundreds of full packing boxes and transform it into a family haven, right down to the framed pictures on the étagères, nearly immediately. "We went before the girls and George, and moved them into this three-story townhouse thing, and in four days we got the whole thing done," said Munn. "We stayed over at the vice president's house, and we had a great time." Over the years, Laura and Lynn did their duo mover routine again and again, for the family's next move, back to Dallas, and for Laura's in-laws, when they moved back to Houston from the White House. It was the kind of whirlwind tour de force you might see on the House & Garden channel these days, one of those specials designed to make the ordinary viewer feel utterly slothful. And this from a woman who also was expert at lying on the sofa for hours with an engrossing book and not moving a muscle.

"I'm sure she hated to leave Midland and her parents and the easy roll of life that she had," said Lynn Munn, "but you would never have known it. That's what they were going to do, and it was seen as something new to do, and she just did it." Her husband threw himself into the thick of his father's campaign as the alter ego of Lee Atwater, the maniacal, brilliant bad boy of GOP strategy. Laura's mother-in-law, the Silver Fox, kept her eye on the entire operation; Bar's political role "was never to be underestimated or ignored, never to be confused with her easygoing public persona," wrote Bill Minutaglio in *First Son.* In Washington, while George plotted, Laura took care of the girls and went to museums. She wandered in galleries. She strolled in gardens. She developed a long-term interest in the antique shops of Georgetown. She had never lived in the East before, and she relished the changing of the seasons, the lush, seductive, fragrant green of spring in Washington, where Lady Bird Johnson had championed the planting of thousands of dogwoods and daffodils. Every Saturday, there were hamburgers for lunch in the vice president's mansion, and the girls raced around, maybe slid down the banister from time to time. While Laura remained at a remove from the daily machinations of the Bush family in full campaign throttle, she was always watching. She was learning. She was always there, certainly; you can see her with her perfect photogenic smile, in the family photo at the 1988 Republican National Convention. George had uprooted the family to Washington without any plan for what he would do after the election. He decided when it was all over, they would move to Dallas. In an interview with the *Houston Chronicle,* he explained that he already was thinking about his own political future. "I want to make it clear that I'm not running for anything right now, but if I do decide to in the future, I'd have to work hard at establishing my own identity," George said. Then he mentioned something that he knew sounded inappropriate as soon as he said it—that he would have a better chance at success if his father lost the presidency. "That is a strange thing to say, isn't it?" he asked. "But if I were to think about running for office and he was president, it would be more difficult to establish my own identity. It probably would help me out more if he lost. He'd be out of politics and be a private citizen. And, you know, people have certain expectations from the son of a president, particularly the oldest one."

And this was the aspect that Laura cared about most of all. She wanted her father-in-law to win his race, certainly. She grew infuriated at what she saw as unsubstantiated attacks against him, particularly the persistent rumors that big George had been unfaithful to Barbara. But what really mattered was whether her husband could build onto the dynasty rather than be stunted by it. "I knew he was going to run again at some point," said Laura, "if ever the timing was right," and then she switched unconsciously into speaking of them as a couple, as one. "We didn't know that his dad would be vice president and president. That kept us from running for a lot of years." After President Bush lost to Bill Clinton in 1992, she said, "George and Jeb were freed, for the first time in their lives, to say what they thought about issues." She might, from time to time, speak of herself and her husband as one, but she would never apply the same responsibilities or freedoms to herself that she had identified for him.

After the family celebrated that first presidential win in 1988 in Houston, they got up the next day and went to church; George W. led the congregation in prayer. Then the family piled onto a military plane and flew to Washington. The seven-year-old twins went wild and rammed toilet paper into the toilet. It fell to the Silver Fox, the new first lady, to fish the sodden masses out of the loo. George would stay through the transition. After the inauguration, Laura and Lynn did their transformative magic act again, and presto! There was a new spacious home for Laura and George in the exclusive Preston Hollow neighborhood in Dallas, not all that far from where Laura had been cosseted at Southern Methodist University. The framed photos went back on the étagère. And a handsome Georgian residence with white pillars and a famous address—1600 Pennsylvania Avenue—was added to the photo collection. Back in Dallas after the inauguration and still functioning as an unofficial adviser to the president and loyalty enforcer, George began planning for his own political future. First, he needed to determine how his candidacy might be perceived not by the voters—they could be won over later—but by any hopeful's first and most important constituency: check writers. He tapped an old Texas friend, a woman who was a longtime high-level Republican operative, and asked her to quietly run his name by some big-money donors. Her reconnaissance report contained some bad news, she later told Bush biographer Minutaglio. She told Bush: "George, everybody likes you, but you haven't done anything. You need to go out in the world and do something, the way that your father did when he left Connecticut and the protection of his family. You just haven't done shit. You're a Bush and that's all."

Well, who didn't like baseball? "George had always dreamed about owning a baseball team," said Laura. "He always wanted to own the Astros. To live in the wall of the Astrodome like Brewster McCloud." But the team for sale was the Texas Rangers, based in Arlington, outside Dallas; the current owner was Eddie Chiles, an old Bush family friend. The baseball commissioner made it clear any new owner would have to have local investment, so George did what he did so well—got on the phone and started selling the deal to investors. His old Yale buddy Roland Betts, now a movie mogul, ponied up some millions, and Bill Dewitt, Bush's old oil partner, got on board. They bought the Rangers for $83 million in April of 1989. All Bush threw in was $500,000, and he funded that with a loan from a Midland bank where he was on the board, using his Harken stock as collateral. The investors agreed that Bush would be managing partner for the team, along with Edward "Rusty" Rose. Bush used his considerable charm to hustle up support for a spanking new stadium, financed on the backs of local taxpayers. And the team began to win games behind the Hall of Fame arm of Nolan Ryan.

George and Laura took the girls to the ballpark lots of nights; eating peanuts and blowing bubble gum, they entertained their Midland friends and newer Dallas associates there. As the daughter-in-law of the president, Laura certainly could have exploded onto the Dallas social scene. But she resisted most attempts to be drawn into that world, populated by rich ladies with their lacquered nails and St. John's knits. Her name did show up from time to time in the society columns of the Dallas papers. She got involved in planning a black-tie fund-raiser for struggling Paul Quinn College, a historically black college in the segregated south side of the city. She addressed invitations for the annual luncheon of the Susan G. Komen Breast Cancer Foundation, which her friend Nancy Brinker had founded in memory of her sister, who died of the disease. Laura preferred the serene, orderly rhythm of the ballpark to the bitchy charity circuit. Over the five years George served as managing partner of the team, she went to some sixty games a year with him, and she found the sport suited her temperament. "It was fun," she said. "Baseball's so slow, you can daydream. It's a very relaxing evening."

While she was daydreaming, George was chattering away at her. "I always say," he wrote in the autobiography, *A Charge to Keep,* "if you're going to a baseball game, you had better go with someone you like, because you have ample time to talk. I went with someone I loved. And talk we did: about baseball, about our girls, about life. . . . Our girls grew up at the ballpark."

The job also gave George the visibility and concrete accomplishment he needed to position himself for a run at governor. He would travel the region talking up the team and the need for the new park. When it finally opened, he and his partners hosted what the *Dallas Morning News* called "an impressive group of VIPs," including financially loaded business chiefs who later were tapped for political donations.

Jenna and Barbara started in Dallas's public schools, but Laura then enrolled them in the Hockaday School, a prestigious all-girls academy. Sundays, the family worshipped at the Highland Park United Methodist Church, which boasted one of the richest congregations in the nation. Periodically, Laura would serve as an Official Bush and representative of the president. She accompanied him and Barbara to the funeral of the legendary Texas senator John Tower and began to assemble a collection of evening gowns for the state dinners her in-laws invited her and George to attend. Sometimes, she even went without him and spent the weekends at Camp David. And while she relished these exclusive events, she often wondered whether they were worth it. During the reelection campaign, George H. W. Bush was being ceaselessly hammered. The Bush family saw most criticism as part of some vast left-wing conspiracy. While candidate Bill Clinton fended off his bimbo problem from the very public claims by Gennifer Flowers, reporters began hearing rumors that George H. W. Bush had a girlfriend, too. Every morning, George and Laura would begin the day the way they always had: She would stay in bed while he went for a run, and then he would bring her coffee and the papers. By 1992, she said, she was "waking up every morning and feeling anxious when George went out to get the newspaper. I'd think, 'What's it going to be today?' It really hurts to see someone you love get attacked. It gets to you after a while."

She felt this anxiety on two fronts: She felt anger over what her family—*her* family, now, these Bushes—had to endure, and she felt apprehension over what she knew was coming for her own life. Her husband never was going to be content just to own a baseball team, that she knew.

Within a few months of quitting drinking that July day in 1986, George had sold off his failing company for fantastic profit. He had moved his family to Washington and become the loyalty enforcer for his father's presidential campaign, a post from which he "earned his spurs" in his father's eyes. "If ever there was competition with his father," said Laura, "it was certainly gone by 1988. . . . He had an opportunity most people never get—to work with his parent as adult to adult. They had time to work through any sort of competition." He had made the keen calculation that he needed to establish a profile for himself apart from the famous surname to make himself electable, and then he had hustled up a group of investors to buy the Texas Rangers and built a spanking new stadium, mostly with public money, outside Dallas. The grandson of a senator and son of a president was thinking of running for governor of Texas and claiming his place in his family's remarkable dynasty. Laura wasn't so sure. She was "always game for anything," as Lynn Munn put it. She liked change. But after a compressed decade of turbulence and two moves, she was content with her life in Dallas, doing her charity work, reading her books, driving her car pools, sitting through the rhythms of inning after inning at the ballpark. She would join him, as always, only after she had ascertained that running for governor was something he truly wanted to do for himself, and not anybody else.

CHAPTER FIVE

The Governor's Wife

I find her to be the perfect wife of a governor.
— George W. Bush, in the *Dallas Morning News*

Being the wife of the governor of Texas, the second most populous state in the union, turned out to be a pretty good first lady starter job. Here's the funny thing about Laura Bush, the shy, ladylike, unobtrusive Laura Bush: She became something of a celebrity first lady of Texas. But this phenomenon happened to her in a gradual, manageable way. When she did her public bits, she got attention; when she went about privately, she found she could travel mostly unnoticed. She could ease into it. It was odd, living in the frontier-style Governor's Mansion in Austin, with vacationers and tourists gawking downstairs, listening to docents drone on about the Texana paintings and the crystal chandelier donated by a sultan and the reasons Sam Houston had been run out of town. It was luxurious, having a hip young cook with a tiny diamond in her nose preparing the family meals. Laura didn't have to drive those twenty car pools a week in Dallas anymore in the Chrysler minivan that George bought her one year for Christmas. But she didn't get to eavesdrop on her girls' chatter in the back seat, revealing that vital intelligence every mother tries to intercept. Most importantly for her promotion to the next unpaid job she would have, first lady of the United States, Laura Bush learned that as first lady of Texas, people would respond to her overtures out of respect for the position itself, no matter what their politics. It wasn't like being the wife of the candidate, bumping and stumping along the back roads and the one-light towns of Texas. And it wasn't like being the daughter-in-law, where you stood in a line smiling with the other adult Bush children, while big George and Bar waved for the camera while the band played, balloons floating to the ceiling and bunting all around.

This time, it was about you.

Laura's friends fretted. "For as long as I've known her," said Regan Gammon, "this is someone who has steadfastly refused to pursue the limelight." The Bushes wondered if their daughter-in-law, so indisputably invaluable behind the scenes in soothing and settling George, could finesse being in full public view.

She had been the last one to sign on to her husband's gubernatorial bid. "I had begun to flirt with the idea," George Bush said, "and Laura was absolutely throwing cold water on it. She was a very reluctant suitor on the subject."

"Our children were little," she said by way of explanation. They were thirteen. And she had a more practical concern: She thought the enormously admired incumbent was unbeatable. Democrat Ann Richards was a shrewd politician with an outsized Texas personality who inspired almost cultlike devotion. "Governor Richards was very popular," said Laura, "and I wasn't really sure how much of a chance George had, at the very first."

"She wanted to make sure this was something I really wanted to do and that I wasn't being drug in as a result of friends, or, well, you're supposed to do it in order to prove yourself, vis-à-vis your father," Bush said.

As was her wont, in considering any changes to her life, Laura took care of her girls and her husband first. Then she got around to taking care of herself. That pattern had been established when she gave up her career at thirty to go off with her husband. It was not that Laura Bush had no sense of self. Rather, she tucked it in the crevices she could find. A few years away from turning fifty, she was at that place and time in life any woman can recognize. Her parents were growing older; back in Midland, her father was afflicted with Alzheimer's disease, and Jenna Welch, who conquered a bout with breast cancer, stoically remained his sole caregiver. Her children were adolescent girls testing their limits, finding their parents embarrassing and dopey on a daily basis. Her husband demanded her emotional energy, and his whole close family was almost turbulent in the charged way they related to one another. The eminently capable Laura balanced all these demands by escaping into her books and retreating with her female friends. A statewide campaign and a stint in the Governor's Mansion seemed to leave precious little time for such pursuits. On top of that, she betrayed some concern about how fulfilling she might find the life of a political wife.

An article in the *Dallas Morning News* several months into Bush's gubernatorial term captured a fascinating exchange between the governor and his wife. Always more garrulous, George had volunteered that "she's having a great time as first lady."

Laura said, less enthusiastically: "It's been a lot better than I expected it to be. In many ways, I thought, 'Oh, gosh, what will I have to do?' "

George said: "Laura was reluctant about whether or not she could carry the banner—giving the speeches and all the stuff she had watched. Frankly, she had watched some darn good people, starting with my mother and father. I'll never forget the big rally we had in Houston. I feature myself as an okay speaker. I feature my mother as a fabulous speaker. And Laura was better than both of us. Remember that day?"

Laura said, with a self-conscious laugh: "It was the first time George ever heard me speak."

George said: "As she gets over worrying about not having the right speech in hand and can ad-lib she's going to be much more comfortable in her role. I find her to be the perfect wife of a governor. Instead of trying to butt in and always, you know, compete. There's nothing worse in the political arena than spouses competing for public accolades or the limelight. And Laura is the perfect complement to a camera hog like me."

I read that back-and-forth between them over and over, trying to tease out their meanings. Neither George nor Laura were ever going to delve into the intricacies of how they related. In my many conversations with Mrs. Bush, when I would attempt to ask how she had adapted to his larger ego, or how she had found a place for herself alongside his ambitions, she would deflect. If the words to explain that were in her emotional vocabulary, if she ever bridled at how he acted as if he owned her feelings, she was not going to share that with the media, and perhaps not even her confidants. I saw him step on her lines many times. She never seemed to mind. Trying to understand the marriage, trying to understand her, was like being an archaeologist sifting through the dust of gestures and the fragments of phrases, attempting to reassemble those pieces into some comprehensible chunk.

Here's what is unclear about their exchange. When she says, "Oh, gosh, what will I have to do?" does she mean she's afraid she won't have anything meaningful or substantive to do in her ceremonial role, that she will be relegated to small talk at luncheons, dressed in silk suits instead of her preferred jeans? Does she mean, "I'm afraid I won't have anything interesting to do?" Or does she mean, "What sort of things will I be called upon to do, in support of my husband, which I find uncomfortable and difficult?" Clearly, the latter is what he took her to mean, and notice how he commandeered her answer. He identified her problem, then solved it for her, and wound up, with a flourish, in saying how good she was for him. He declared, not too subtly, how preferable her style was to say, oh, let's just name her, Hillary Rodham Clinton, at that time, in 1995, firmly enmeshed in power struggles between the East and West wings. But the whole exchange wound up being about him, Governor Bush, and his perceptions of her experience, didn't it?

Once they were installed in the Governor's Mansion in Austin, their marriage seemed to settle into a pattern. His inclination was to race ahead toward some new goal, straining against the lead. Her role was to pull him back a bit, check his speed, and make sure he was being considered, not impetuous. Her inclination was to hug the wall, observing from the outskirts of the room. His role was to make her comfortable in continuing in that vein, rather than encouraging her to exploit her considerable smarts. He offered no push to match her pull. Just the opposite.

"I knew she was uncertain about moving to Austin," George said. "She was a little fearful, maybe, about whether any of this life would be to her liking. So my attitude was, 'Laura, if you want to sit in the Governor's Mansion during my term in office, that's fine with me. You and the girls didn't ask to be put in this position, and I promise I'm not going to make any of you do anything.'"

I'm not going to make any of you do anything.

In the end Laura did do something. "I finally said, 'Well, if I'm going to be a public figure, I might as well do what I've always liked doing,'" Laura recalled, "which meant acting like a librarian and getting people interested in reading."

"Yeah, she picked a cause, and that's what so smart for anybody to do," said Liz Carpenter, an Austin resident who had served as press secretary to Lady Bird Johnson and aide to Lyndon Johnson. "That way, you have some sort of identity instead of doing whatever little thing people asked her to do—like Pat Nixon running to a hospital here and disturbing sick children there."

As her first effort, during the inaugural week Laura hosted a reading by Texas authors, a format she would repeat in Constitution Hall in Washington when her husband was sworn in as the forty-third president of the United States. She began to travel across the state speaking up on behalf of literacy and early reading programs. The inevitable comparisons to Barbara Bush began, since literacy had been her issue as well. Laura stood her ground and made the rare public statement of identity apart from the clan. "I didn't want to step on Bar's issue," said Laura, "but it had also been my issue long before I became a Bush. And I think that Bar loved what I was doing." She always would smoothly evade any suggestion of conflict between her and her mother-in-law. Laura actually seemed to enjoy Bar's feisty competiveness. Years later, after she had become first lady, Laura told Bar that a school near Austin had been named for her—the first—and Bar said, "I have six."

The Austin intellectual crowd first snapped to attention during that initial inaugural event, which took place the day before her husband's January 17, 1995, swearing-in. Laura asked authors who were self-described progressives to read—and rocked them back on their heels. Even the invitation to the event itself, at the Humanities Center of the University of Texas, caused quite the ruckus, recalled Stephen Harrigan, author of the historical novel *The Gates of the Alamo.* Several of those invited to attend "were genuinely perplexed," said Harrigan. They might be intellectuals, but the writers lived in a political town, and they immediately grasped that their new first lady was setting a tone and making a statement with her first event, although the local press mostly ignored the reading amid the swirl of the entire inaugural weekend. "The writers' attitude was sort of a deer-in-the-headlights quality," said Harrigan. "A Republican first lady? Should I go to that? Is it right? Such a thing had never happened before. Even Democrats didn't invite writers to the mansion."

The night before the event, she dreamed she was sinking in Styrofoam. "I knew I was going to have to speak at the reading, and I thought that the writers may not have voted for George," she said. "So I had an anxiety dream." Instead, before she read, novelist Sarah Bird stood and said, "I just have to say how impressed I am y'all would invite a raging liberal like me. It gives me a lot of hope for this administration." The group represented a breadth of genre and geography: There was historian T. R. Fehrenbach from San Antonio and San Angelo's Elmer Kelton, who had written scores of Wild West novels, mystery writer Mary Willis Walker, and author and *New Yorker* writer Lawrence Wright, from Austin, among others.

Laura herself spoke very briefly, saying that she hoped to organize literary readings at the Governor's Mansion. She had invited some of her former teaching colleagues from Dawson Elementary School, and she told the gathering that she also hoped to focus on programs such as Head Start, for at-risk children. At that first event, she saw a pathway: Her position created opportunities and permitted associations outside strictly Republican circles, as long as she didn't do anything to discredit her husband. "Even if the writers had not voted for him," she said later, "they were glad to do it for Texas as opposed to for a candidate."

Some months later, after she had arranged life in the Governor's Mansion to her liking, and installed the twins in private St. Andrew's Episcopal School, Laura embarked on her most ambitious project—the Texas Book Festival. An annual free weekend of readings and author appearances, the festival secured Laura Bush's legacy in her state and earned her loyalty. With its reputation as a rambunctious, rough-edged cowboy state, Texas had suffered mightily on a national level with the arts-and-letters crowd. In the popular mind, there was James Michener, who didn't even live in Texas, and there was Larry McMurtry. Other writers published in relative obscurity.

Here again, initially, the state's writers and intellectuals, many of them affiliated with the University of Texas, were taken aback by Laura Bush. Laura was absolutely right: Few of them had voted for her husband, who became only the second Republican in the state's governor's office since Reconstruction. They were appalled that Shrub, as acerbic columnist Molly Ivins dubbed him, had commandeered their state capital. Most of the Austin literary crowd had no knowledge of Laura's years at Dawson Elementary, in the poor, pocked Hispanic southwest corner of the city. To them, she was just another helmet-haired Republican wife.

When she plunged into organizing the first festival, however, "it quickly became apparent that this wasn't some first lady enthusiasm," said Harrigan. "It was a serious attempt, and she was in charge. She knew what she wanted. She wanted four people to read—she liked the idea of readings rather than speeches—and she pushed to get the state capitol," which all agreed was a phenomenal location, with its majestic pink granite rotunda rising high off Capitol Street. "And the authors we were talking about, down to the most obscure, she had read their works and could discuss them."

He admits he was surprised by that; others were outright shocked. Laura, like her husband, excelled compared to preconceived low expectations. Don McLeese, assigned to cover the glittering black-tie fund-raising gala that opened the festival, wrote in the *Austin American-Statesman* that he "figured it would be an elitist snoozefest. Just what Texas literature needs: a bunch of corporate sponsors paying high-dollar tribute to books they haven't read, while authors enjoy (endure?) the rare opportunity to dress like penguins and be treated like movie stars—all for the sake of giving the state's first lady a higher profile and a sense of public mission. Plant a tree for Lady Bird Johnson, just say no for Nancy Reagan, and read a book for Laura Bush. Whenever government and rich folks join hands, no matter how noble the aspiration, my populist instinct is to watch my wallet and look for the ulterior motive."

McLeese found no ulterior motive. Instead, he came away moved by the fellowship of readers and writers. Before the gala, Larry McMurtry said, "Reading is one of the stablest and cheapest pleasures of life, and it's also one of the most liberating." Larry L. King, best known as the playwright of *The Best Little Whorehouse in Texas,* talked about how growing up poor in West Texas "the public library saved my life." Sandra Cisneros divulged that the only book in her Mexican-American home when she was growing up was a Bible, redeemed with Green Stamps. "We are here to rejoice in the abundance and variety of Texas literature," said Laura Bush, "one of Texas's most significant resources, one that helped shape our identity and chartered our course."

She had worried over the festival, which was nearly a year in the planning. "Oh, gosh! What if it's just us and the 250 volunteers?" she said. Instead, thousands thronged the capitol grounds, standing in lines to speak with authors and get books signed. The festival generated more than $260,000 in revenue, from sales of books, T-shirts and tote bags, a silent auction and the gala.

Each year the festival has grown; it now is considered one of the premier literary events of the Southwest. By 2002, more than seven hundred authors had participated, and the event had contributed $1.43 million to Texas public libraries. That money is critical. While Laura Bush worked hard to raise funds for public libraries through the festival, she certainly did not have any success in increasing legislative funding for the institutions she considered vitally important: Texas ranks forty-third in the nation in funding for public libraries. A fact sheet from the Texas Book Festival revealed a stunning statistic: A $2,500 festival grant "typically doubles the annual materials budget of a public library," meaning each year, those libraries which had "saved" the young Larry L. King had only $1,250 to buy new books and replace old ones.

When I talked to the people in Austin involved in the festival, all of them made it clear that Laura Bush actually had worked, not served as some ceremonial figurehead. They also made it clear they had fallen in love with her, no matter what her husband's politics. She was universally admired.

"She was very involved with author selection," said Mary Margaret Farabee, the festival's executive director since its inception. "She helped pick them, and she signed all the letters and everything.

She came to every meeting," most of which were at the home of Regan Gammon, who chaired the author selection committee for the festival's first four years, and who invited Laura to join her women's book club in Austin. Said Harrigan, also an organizer, "Laura wouldn't run the meeting in a directed way, but you were always aware that her opinions were well informed. She had opinions about certain writers, and how an event should be set up. People would turn to her and say, 'Can you write a letter? Can you do this and that?' And she was just interested in every aspect of it. She picked up the phone a lot to get things done. She'd call me if she had a question and say, 'Hi, this is Laura.' "

It is her signature style, an unaffected, informal, friendly directness. Among political figures, that style is highly unusual. Former Labor Secretary Robert Reich once had an advance man named Ken Sain who carefully schooled the secretary on the fine points of being a "muck," a muckety-muck. In Reich's memoir, *Locked in the Cabinet,* Sain laid it out for his boss: A muck doesn't carry bags. A muck doesn't dawdle and wait for others to catch up. A muck is always in the photograph. A muck always arrives a few minutes late.

Laura Bush is absolutely incapable of being a muck.

While her new position required that she travel about with a Department of Public Safety trooper, she seemed to savor the relative anonymity she had when her husband wasn't by her side. She would hop on and off Southwest Airlines and visit her girlfriends around the state. Each morning, she would walk with her trooper from her capitol office to the basement cafeteria for coffee. One day, as she stood in line to pay for her cup, the man in front of her noticed the trooper. "I wonder who's in here?" the man asked her. "I don't know," she replied. Several times a month, she would put on her sneakers and walk out the back door of the mansion and head for Regan's house two miles away, through the University of Texas campus and a park. On one of those walks, waiting for the light to change, Laura recognized Christina Huegel, a UT student who was interning in the governor's office. They fell in step, and Laura walked with her all the way, chitchatting with the young woman about her classes and her experiences. "That's just the kind of person she is," said Charlene Fern, Mrs. Bush's speechwriter in Austin and in the White House, who told me that story. "I remember how blown away by that Chrissy was, that she would just walk along with her for two miles." One day, when Laura was shopping with the twins at Wal-Mart, a woman with her in the checkout line kept questioning her—"You look so familiar, why do you look so familiar?" until Laura gave her name. "Sorry," said the woman, "that doesn't ring a bell," and Laura and the girls laughed and laughed later.

She would slip into functions rather than making entrances. People would gasp with surprise when they realized she was sitting next to them at some event. At parties she and the governor gave at the mansion, she liked to be outside with the dogs. "But people gravitated to her," said Paul Burka, the *Texas Monthly* writer. "She loved to talk about the dogs."

"She doesn't work a room," says Farabee. "She just wants to talk to whoever is there, and really talk to them, you know? She focuses on you. She doesn't want to draw attention to herself, which is just so amazing. She is just . . . real."

During the six years George Bush spent as governor of Texas, ordering the executions of more death row prisoners than any governor before him, publicly affirming the state's sodomy laws, people who knew Laura socially or worked with her on projects came to assume she was far more liberal than her husband. There was never any hard evidence for this; Laura always was very careful to sidestep any political or social questions outside her carefully focused issues. It was all circumstantial.

"She knows what her role is, and she expresses her feelings privately," asserted Eddie Safady, the president of Liberty Bank in downtown Austin and a civic leader. "She does what she can. I think she is a very smart woman who has observed things from first ladies. And I think George is a very likable man, if you divorce him from his politics. I imagine they have some pretty interesting conversations behind closed doors." And this was a typical view, which neither Laura nor George and his political backers refuted. It worked for the Republicans to have Laura seen as some sort of compassionate and moderating influence. She could appeal to middle-of-the-road voters, soccer moms, so much so that Republican National Committee chair Haley Barbour brought her in to deliver a prime-time speech at the 1996 convention in San Diego.

People counted on Laura never to let George drift too far to the right, and this belief in her persisted, without a single example to prop it up. The argument went something like this: "I know he can't be that reactionary deep down, because Laura wouldn't be married to someone like that," and I heard versions of this often from hopeful social liberals in Austin and in Washington.

Part of these assumptions came from Laura's librarian background, and people speculated she maintained the librarian's libertarian philosophy. She certainly had the open mind of one. "She's not walled off in any sort of intellectual sense," Harrigan observed, "nor is she scared of ideas." Partly, it was her catholic taste in reading. She would read anything. She loved difficult, challenging literary fiction, particularly novels that probed the dark corners of the human mind and soul. She had been raised a Democrat. And, "all her best friends are Democrats, you know," said her rascal pal Kinky Friedman, the outrageous, foul-mouthed, self-anointed "Texas Jew Boy." Most of her friends are pro-choice, pro–gun control, pro-environment, classically liberal. In addition to her work with the festival, Regan is an active preservationist in Austin and a trustee for the Episcopal Seminary of the Southwest, which proudly announced its position against the war in Iraq by posting several snapshots of its faculty and students hoisting placards at an Austin peace rally. Jane Fontenot had unassailable progressive credentials: She was a midwife in Berkeley. Mary Margaret Farabee was married to a former Democratic state legislator, a devoted *New Yorker* magazine reader who nearly wept with joy the day the *New York Times* went national and she could get home delivery. Bibliophile that she is, Laura preferred to surround herself with writers and artists, people who created work that was not readily accessible to the masses or even popular. She became friends with several gay men and went antiquing with them. She would poke around in secondhand shops in all sorts of seedy neighborhoods, eat in any manner of cheap Mexican restaurants. "You'd walk into the most unlikely dive, and there her picture would be, under the glass," her friend Adair Margo said.

Political views rarely were offered or requested in discussions with Laura. "You just didn't go there," said Farabee. "I've never talked politics with her," said Harrigan. "I think she could surprise you." Lynn Munn, her old friend from Midland, had a habit of shaking her finger in the governor's face about gun control when she and her husband, Bill, came down to Austin. And Laura would just ease things for her with George by saying, "You know Lynn, her idea of gun control is that nobody should have one," and they all would laugh. It was a reporter's question about the death penalty that brought Laura's retort, "If I differ from my husband, I'm not going to tell you."

She cleaved to her girlfriends, and they offered her sanctuary. When the Bushes socialized personally, rather than politically, they did so with her friends and their husbands. She was a faithful attendee at the book group that Regan invited her to join; it was as much a social gathering as a literary discussion. And she was an attentive friend, amid the ribbon cuttings and cafeteria duty at the girls' school and political functions in her own home. When one of the club members was well enough to return to the book club after a long absence due to cancer, Laura called her up and diplomatically inquired, "Can I come pick you up?" She didn't want her friend to have to go alone.

Laura's own instinct for survival let her know when she needed to get away from her jobs as wife and mother and first lady. She would call up one of her girlfriends and say, "I'm coming over." They'd sit and have a glass of wine, and Laura would smoke a couple of cigarettes. She began going on a retreat with her friends every summer, hiking or rafting in the West. She explored friendships with authors she met, and they welcomed her into their realm.

On a visit to a ranch outside Austin where the short-story writer Lee Byrd was on fellowship, Laura and Lee went hiking in the heat, then decided to jump into the swollen Barton Creek and get refreshed. The impromptu plunge left Laura's panicked trooper scrambling to keep his gun dry. "She may have hesitated for about three seconds," said Margo, who was along, "then it was like, plop. All the way."

"She was laughing, because her hair got wet and she was worried her roots would show, all these funny, girl things," remembers Byrd. While their underwear dried in the sun, the women ate blueberry pie with their fingers and talked about books.

If she advised her husband, Laura did so privately. She worked from a small office in the basement of the capitol. She had one staffer, Andrea Ball, the wife of a water-well-drilling company owner, who did everything from answering the phone to sending letters and helping schedule appointments. Andi had been the administrative assistant in charge of the office of the state Republican Party when Karen Hughes was executive director. She had been an aide to Phil Gramm when he was in Congress. After Bush was elected governor, Andi worked on his inaugural and then landed a job in the governor's office handling his mail. The first lady seemed solicitous of Andi, who had no college degree, and made sure she was treated with respect.

"She was protective of Andi," remembers Terral Smith, who was Bush's legislative director, his liaison to the Texas House and Senate. "I remember we were going to [Democratic House speaker]

Pete Laney's mother's funeral, she and Andi and [Bush chief of staff] Joe Albaugh and me, and there were but three first-class tickets. And she said, firmly, 'Andi sits up here with me.' She didn't want her off in the back while we were all up front. And I thought that was proper and good, and so I sat back there in coach."

But while she represented her husband, in her gracious way, in such official capacities, Laura had no political strategists or policy advisers. If any reporter asked about Laura's ambitions, in those years when Hillary Clinton was blazing trails as a political wife, Laura demurred that she had no interest in having input into policy. When Paul Burka asked if she ever would lobby legislators to vote for a certain bill, she appeared startled, he wrote. "Well, no," she answered him. "The idea hasn't occurred to me."

Yes, she thought teachers deserved better pay. Yes, she thought more money should be spent on reading programs. No, she was not about to persuade her husband to increase aid. As usual, George answered for her—and was more revealing than she ever would be. "She knows that the literacy program is not so much about spending money as it is focusing on how the money that we have is being spent," the governor said. "Look, Laura and I read the paper together every morning, and we discuss different issues. She's always asking what I'm going to be doing about this and that. But I think she trusts me to make the right decision." This was a pattern she would carry to the White House, in which she seemed almost actively to cover her tracks. It was the political equivalent of her more personal lobbying—whether to get him to quit drinking or curb his tongue. When I interviewed her for the first time, the month after George W. Bush was sworn in as president, I asked her to talk about what she had done for education in Texas. Her press secretary, Noelia Rodriguez, had to prompt her. "Tell her about the money you got the legislature to put in," Rodriguez said. "Oh, there were a lot of people involved," said Mrs. Bush. It was so curious, to hear this modesty from a woman now installed in the White House, in a city where the prevailing political posture was a pompous "don't you know who I am?"

Others in Texas readily acknowledged that Laura had a voice in education policy. Months before she told Burka that it had never occurred to her to lobby legislators, she in fact had actively influenced adoption of some early education reforms. Laura held a conference for the lawmakers and reached out to some important Democrats—and this netted $215 million in new programs for reading readiness. "We simply knew it was Laura Bush's bill," said Paul Sadler, a Democrat who chaired the House education committee. "She was very much at the forefront, and knew the subject very well."

Her activity was a departure from the tradition of the women who had preceded her, no matter what Laura said. "I did not lobby on my own or sponsor any legislation," said former first lady of Texas Rita Clements, whose husband, Bill Clements, had preceded Ann Richards as governor. And Nellie Connally, the wife of former Governor John Connally, who served from 1963 to 1969, "tended to things that were my duty," like gardening and making a home for her family. Back then, a governor's wife would be seen "as getting in where she shouldn't get in" if she directly engaged in getting bills passed, said Connally.

In a speech she delivered to a group of Republican women in 2000, when her husband was running for president, Laura appealed, again, to the compassion and populism of party moderates: The words "no child left behind" cropped up. Time and again, using words she had worked on with her speechwriter Charlene Fern, Laura would recount how her mother, Jenna Welch, had read to her as a child, then smoothly segue into a plea:

"Not every child is so fortunate. Many enter school without even knowing such basics as the alphabet or their colors or how to count to ten. For these children, reading and learning can be a struggle. And if they don't get help early, then theirs becomes a lifetime of playing catch-up, or giving up, or dropping out. These same faces, that started out with such high hopes, wind up in prisons and welfare lines and homeless shelters. That's why George began his mission to make sure that every child is educated and that no child is left behind. It's why he pushed for more money and resources so teachers can help children learn regardless of their abilities when they started school.

"My experience as a mom and as an elementary school teacher taught me how smart children really are, how eager they are to learn, and how easily we can fail them, at home and at school, if we don't have high expectations and high standards." She always would include, to great effect, some anecdotes directly from the mouths of children: "Listen to what some fourth-graders recently wrote to George and me in their essays titled, 'What I Have Learned.' Ten-year-old Melissa wanted us to know that if you catch a catfish, don't swing it around." (Laughter.) "Nine-year-old Joshua said that he had learned that it doesn't matter how people look on the outside; it's the inside that counts." (Applause.) "And this from Tiffany: Parents know spinach isn't good for you; they just like that expression on your face." (Laughter.)

When she launched an early reading initiative, "Ready to Read," the legislature funded it for $17 million, which was $15 million more than the $2 million she had requested, through the governor's office, and it became the first state appropriation ever to local Head Start programs, funded federally.

"I always had a first lady amendment" going, said Smith, the legislative director. "There would always be two or three things" she would be working on, he said, usually with input from Bush's director of social policy, Margaret LaMontagne Spellings, who later became his domestic policy adviser in the White House. "I think she was very influential with him, especially on education."

If he was the governor of the state, Laura remained the governor of George Bush. He was dependent on her. His scheduler knew to get him home at night, back to the house, whenever possible. He hated being somewhere else overnight. When he got too wound up about something, Laura would give George a look, rein him in. He would get too gregarious; she would say, quietly, "You're talking too much." Smith recalls the days when George was already running for president and the three of them had attended a San Antonio rally.

"He was high. He was feeling good. There had been like, five hundred screaming supporters, and on the way back, he was telling me how he was going to appoint me to head some agency, with the election a month out, and I was a little interested. And Laura put her hand on his knee and said, 'Yes, George, but I think that's a little premature.' "

In the late summer months of the 2000 presidential campaign, the race between Bush and Al Gore tightened. The vice president got a much-needed bounce from the Democratic convention, and a whiff of desperation began to float over the governor's campaign. He was flubbing his words more and more. "Bush is knocked off his message, and the timing couldn't be worse," NBC's David Gregory ominously reported in September. Laura had been maintaining her own separate campaign schedule for much of the summer. Bush's advisers huddled and realized they needed to get her on his plane. He was too jittery otherwise. Independently, Laura had been watching her husband on television clips between her own stops. She had come to the same conclusion.

"She has a really good sense of how he is doing," said Mark McKinnon, the Austin media adviser who frequently traveled on the campaign. "She's the first one to hear the creaks in the submarine when it goes too low."

Once Laura was back on board, McKinnon saw the difference, he told Burka later. "She brought calm and serenity to his bearing. He was happier, more at ease, less distracted. . . . If she wasn't there, he'd bounce around the plane."

But when she was there, he could play his favorite game, teasing her. It went like this: Laura would try to read her book. George would try to get her attention, using the nickname they had for each other. "Bushie"—poke with his finger—"Bushie"—poke— "Bushie"—poke, until she looked up with exasperation and weary amusement. "What, George?" she would say, and then he'd blurt out some dumb thing. She'd return to her book. Twenty seconds later he would start again: "Bushie"—poke. Another time, he joked that he had so much fried food at a campaign event in West Texas that he was going to have to let a big one fly. "Oh, no you're not," she said. "Oh, yes, I am," he countered, with a big grin on his face. He was like a hyperactive little boy, but he seemed to need these escapades to remove his stress, keep him focused when the time came to rouse himself for one more rally in one more state.

Later, once they were all safely moved into the White House, Bush aides agreed that Laura's decision to come aboard the plane marked the turning point in his comeback. For the second time, she had become the person most responsible for making that man president of the United States. "She is," said McKinnon, "his safety net for life."

The comfort of their Austin life was plunged into chaos the minute the polls closed on November 7, 2000, and it didn't end until the Supreme Court effectively granted Bush the presidency thirty-three days later. Team Bush was frantic through the holiday season, in constant contact with lawyers in Florida, monitoring every fit and start in the court actions, listening to acrimony build among voters of both parties.

Amidst all that, Laura opened another Texas Book Festival. When she rose to speak, people sat paralyzed, wondering how she was doing, what she would say. Laura looked as calm as she always did. "Welcome to the Texas Book Festival," she said, "an event whose outcome is never in doubt." The audience laughed with relief. "I promise you won't hear the word 'recount,' " she added, and smiled.

On the day after the court delivered its ruling, and Gore got ready to concede, and her husband prepared to deliver his long-delayed acceptance speech, the festival was holding its scheduled wrap-up meeting between 5:30 and 7:00 P.M. Nobody expected Laura to be there, given the day's stunning news developments. Her husband and Dick Cheney and Condoleezza Rice were upstairs at the mansion, getting ready for the televised address. Laura left the residence and went to the festival meeting, right on time.

"Think about this!" recalled Harrigan. "Her husband was going to his acceptance speech, and at that very moment of this unprecedented election being decided, history was about to change. Her life was about to change. And she was sitting there listening to how many T-shirts we had sold, and asking were those tote bags moving well, because we would need to order them again. I remember sitting there and thinking, 'Wow, this is remarkable,' not just on a level of compartmentalization, but on a level of fundamental courtesy to all these volunteers who had worked so long and so hard to make that festival happen. She was sending a signal that this was just as important as anything going on with the election.

"I thought that was a very revealing and interesting moment."

She left the meeting and went back to her home of the past six years, and readied herself to become the first lady of the United States. She had come to love her life in Austin. With her friendly, low-key manner, people had come to treat her the way she liked best, as "just Laura." Her best friend was nearby, as was Jenna, at the University of Texas. Her mother was a drive away. Someone once asked her if she had lost herself in the clutter of ribbon cuttings and day-care center visits, and she had said, surprised, "No, I've found myself." In the long months of discussion with her husband and daughters about whether he should run for president of the United States, she had argued forcefully against it, and foremost in her reasoning was losing "the freedom of being able to move around without starting up a motorcade."

And now here she came in one, motorcycles revving, sirens blaring, lights flashing. One of the couple's last social outings in Austin was to Tracy and Greg Curtis's Christmas party. Greg was editor of *Texas Monthly*; Tracy was in Laura's book club, and the Bushes had gone every year. This December, everybody attending froze for a minute when they heard the unusual racket. Then they realized: Their old friends were coming in this long, screeching motorcade. It was precisely the sort of entrance Laura hated.

That night, Paul Burka asked her how she felt about moving on. He remembered how he would run into her on Congress Avenue, standing in line at the post office or the drugstore.

"Well," Laura said, ruefully, "I guess I won't be running out the back door of the White House to the Rexall anymore."

CHAPTER SIX

❧

The White House

She cuts right through the posturing and positioning. America's starved for something. I'm telling you: They're starved for something real. And that's what she brings. She's a real person.

—George W. Bush, in the *New York Times*

Laura and George W. Bush landed in the White House in one of the most controversial elections in American history. Nevertheless, their arrival was accompanied by all the traditional pomp and flourish that America musters when installing a new leader. This time Texans wore boots under their ball gowns, and a former president wiped a tear as he watched his son sworn in. Laura Bush stepped into her job in her cautious, almost unobtrusive way. Everybody wanted to know: What's she *really* like? They thought they knew her husband; gregarious, quick, impatient, decisive, bombastic George. They might hate him, or they might love him—the country was bitterly divided, and the sour taste of the most disputed election in a century would linger all through his first term—but they knew him. Laura remained enigmatic anywhere outside Texas. Despite her well-received addresses at the Republican National Conventions in 1996 and 2000 and her own spate of campaign appearances, her characteristic reticence made her opaque. Always best and most comfortable relating to people one on one, Laura struggled with projecting her "something real" through the media or to the back of a crowded ballroom. Most of the time, she didn't even bother to try. Long before, her husband had set the bar for her performance very low. *"You and the girls didn't ask to be put in this position, and I promise I'm not going to make any of you do anything."*

"What's she *really* like?" people would ask me again and again, after I had started to cover her for the *Washington Post.* Behind the smiling, impassive mask she presented to the public, standing a step behind her husband, was she some kind of Stepford Wife, a throwback to those dutiful shirtwaists of the 1950s, who drowned their boredom in one too many through the day? Or was she a thoroughly modern woman? As if anybody knew what *that* really meant. Was she publicly genteel and privately tart? Smarter than he? Better read? Did she work to make herself deliberately smaller? A stealth adviser, influential behind the scenes, or a dutiful helpmeet, fading into the background? Was she like Nancy Reagan, suspected of using her better intellect to really run the West Wing? Was she like her own mother-in-law, reassuringly matronly but full of wicked barbs? And thank *God,* people would say, isn't it a relief to have someone like Laura in there, after this last one? "I admire Hillary, I guess," one longtime White House observer said to me, "but really, wasn't she a bit much?" Laura, it was implied, knew her place.

And what is that place? The job has that peculiar title. Linger over it when you say it—First. Lady.—to truly appreciate how out-of-date it is. The position is purely derivative. All reflected power. There is no job description, no constitutional mandate, no clear set of performance goals. The American people are fairly clear about what they expect from their president, and every four years, they have a chance to make a new hire. They are far more ambiguous about what they want from the man's wife.

In years past, she was expected only to be gracious hostess and well-mannered companion, a woman capable of discoursing with the French president at a state dinner and charming tots at the Easter Egg Roll. She was responsible for the culture of the White House in those decades before we even knew every institution was supposed to have "a culture"—the culture of the workplace, the culture of the Senate, the culture of the Junior League. But those earlier expectations of first ladyship have gone the way of the Miss America Pageant—looking lovely and walking properly is no longer enough. Now, the first lady must roll out substantive, meaningful issues, which must never conflict with or overshadow those of her husband's administration, yet none of the traditional duties may be removed from her list. "The problem with being first lady is that it's a lot like being Caesar's wife," said Patricia Schroeder, the former Democratic representative from Colorado. "If you don't do anything, you are too bland. If you do something, you are too strident. I don't envy anyone who has that role."

The modern first lady must not appear too vigorous in her efforts to leverage her remarkable recognizability into accomplishment; Hillary Rodham Clinton is the lesson here, a woman who caused plenty of observers to positively recoil when she wielded her power too transparently. Being first lady is "really a complicated calculation. It's very difficult," Clinton told me, once she had moved into the relative freedom of the United States Senate. "You are probably going to disappoint and alienate half of the people . . . All you can do is be yourself. That is what I tried to do. People agree and disagree and project on you all their expectations, but at the end of the day, you have to live with yourself."

It's a horrible job, actually, but the first lady must never complain, lest she be seen as ungrateful for all the fabulous perquisites that come her way—the box at the Kennedy Center, the trips on *Air Force One,* the tour of the Louvre on the day it is closed. It's all such a *privilege.*

And: The modern first lady must do something that establishes her as having her own identity, because in America in the twenty-first century, a woman must aspire to more than wifehood and motherhood. As Sarah Wildman wrote in the *New Republic,* "Before feminism, [the job] was brutally constricting; today, it's simply impossible." The president's wife who refused to do this would be a liability. In a *Today* show interview that aired a few hours before the inauguration, Katie Couric said to Laura, "You appear to be a very traditional woman. Is that a fair characterization?"

"I don't think that's really exactly fair," Laura replied. "I've had traditional—jobs that were traditionally women's jobs. I've been a teacher, I've been a librarian. I had the luxury of staying home and raising my children when I had children. That was really what I wanted to do, was to be at home with them. But I also think that I've been a very contemporary woman in a lot of ways. I had a career for a number of years. I didn't marry George until I was in my thirties. I worked on issues always that are very, very important to me, either working as a teacher or librarian or working as a volunteer or working as the first lady of my state. And so I think I'm both ways."

Yet this emphasis on independence paradoxically has denigrated the most important and powerful role our first ladies have—as provider of sustenance, advice, love, and support to the man in the Oval Office. Their influence often is overlooked when historians turn their attention to America's past presidents. Pick up a biography of Roosevelt or Wilson or Reagan, and thumb through the index; the number of pages devoted to an examination of the presidential marriage and its impact on governance ranges from slight to nonexistent.

"The most confident presidents generally have been those with the healthiest respect for their wives, men who sought and listened to their wives' personal and political advice," concluded Kati Marton, after studying twelve presidential marriages for her book *Hidden Power.* She noted that "the institution's outer face has never been

Laura graduates from Southern Methodist University in 1968, with a bachelor's degree in elementary education. *Southern Methodist University*

After their simple wedding on November 5, 1977, the bride and groom line up with the Bush clan outside First United Methodist Church in Midland. Never much interested in clothes, Laura wore a two-piece dress she bought off the rack in Austin. *George Bush Presidential Library*

Laura was "just born a happy little kiddo," her mother, Jenna Welch, once said of her only child. *Family photo*

Hugging a new doll under the Christmas tree in 1950. Without siblings, Laura lined up her dolls and taught them. *Family photo*

Two-year-old Laura sits with her dog, Bully, and her maternal grandfather, Harold Hawkins, on the front steps of his home in El Paso. Hawkins was a character, fond of having Texas Select bourbon for breakfast once in a while. *Family photo*

George and Laura Bush in 1979, in a Midland backyard. After George lost his congressional race, he went back to being an independent oilman, and Laura kept house. *Family photo*

The newlyweds campaign for Congress from the back of a flatbed pickup. Laura regards those long months on the road as a great adventure, which gave the two of them time to know each other intimately. *Family photo*

An exhausted and ecstatic George Bush holds his newborns on November 25, 1981. "I got weepy," he said, when he showed the twins to Laura in the operating room. "And then I realized that our life had changed forever in a positive way." *George Bush Presidential Library*

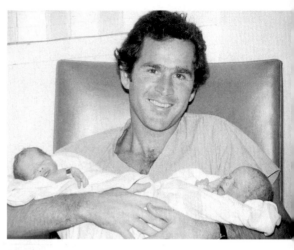

The new mother with her five-week-old babies on New Year's Day, 1982. Laura loved dusk in her garden, after she had safely tucked the twins into bed. *Family photo*

George and Laura Bush pose with Barbara and Jenna on vacation in Maine, back when the twins were pliant enough to wear what their mother wanted. *George Bush Presidential Library*

A rare moment: Laura is at the mike taking questions from the audience during a presidential campaign appearance in 2000, while the candidate stands behind her, watching. *Rick Wilking/REUTERS*

George and Laura, in her preferred outfit of shirt and jeans, at their 1,583-acre ranch in Crawford. Laura was very involved in the designing and building of their modest home there, and she has made it a priority to maintain the ranch as a retreat from the pressures of the presidency. *AP/Wide World Photos*

Even in her demanding years in the White House, Laura Bush has stayed connected to her closest women friends, most of whom grew up with her in Midland. Each year, they try to take a weeklong vacation together. Here, the women pose for a snapshot during a 1996 Utah rafting trip. *From left,* Jane Ann Fontenot, Regan Gammon, Peggy Weiss, Laura, and, in front, Marge Petty.

Laura hugs Barbara good-bye at the Governor's Mansion in Austin, November 10, 2000. Friends in Austin were astonished at how calm Laura remained during the tumultuous 36-day battle that followed Election Day 2000. "Politics doesn't totally consume her," George once said, "and as a result, it doesn't totally consume me." *Jeff Haynes/AFP/Getty Images*

Good-bye to Midland: Before flying off on *Air Force One* to a weekend of inaugural festivities, the Bushes paid tribute to their West Texas roots with an exuberant rally in their hometown. © *Tribune Media Services, Inc. All Rights Reserved. Reprinted with permission.*

Barbara, Jenna, and Laura beam on stage at the Florida State Inaugural Ball on January 20, 2001. The Bushes attended eight different balls to celebrate the historic event; George W. Bush was only the second son of a president to ascend to the office. *Larry Downing/REUTERS*

President and Laura Bush attend the opening ceremonies for the maiden National Book Festival in September 2001. The first lady and her staff began planning the event, modeled after a similar book festival she organized in Texas, even before the inauguration. *Lois Raimondo/*The Washington Post

Laura, in a vibrant red and hot pink Arnold Scaasi gown, stands with the president in the North Portico of the White House, awaiting the arrival of Mexican President Vicente Fox and his wife, Martha, at the Bushes' first state dinner on September 5, 2001. The glittering party and the successful literary festival a week later, said Laura, had represented "what I thought it would be like to be the wife of the president, to live in the White House." *Mike Theiler/ AFP/Getty Images*

With her Secret Service agents nearby, Laura Bush watches from the West Wing colonnade as Presidents Bush and Fox answer reporters' questions in the Rose Garden. The first lady carefully monitors how her husband's tone and temperament are projecting in public. *Rich Lipski/*The Washington Post

Flanked by emergency workers outside Walter Reed Army Medical Center, Laura talks about visiting with victims of the Pentagon attacks. At left is the hospital's commander, General Harold L. Timboe. *Susan Biddle*/The Washington Post

Her face lined with pain, Laura, with Pennsylvania Governor Tom Ridge, speaks to reporters after a September 17, 2001, memorial service for victims of the United Flight 93 crash. In the days following the attacks, she quickly became the nation's comforter-in-chief. *Jason Cohn/REUTERS*

The first couple with the first dogs, Springer spaniel, Spot and that rascally Scottie, Barney. The president jokes that Barney is "the son he never had," but the terrier is really Laura's. He gave him to her for her birthday in 2000. *Stephen Jaffe/AFP/Getty Images*

On Capitol Hill, Laura delivers the education testimony that had been interrupted by the September 11 attacks. She became only the fourth first lady to testify on the Hill, and certainly the only one whose audience of senators included the first lady who immediately preceded her, Hillary Rodham Clinton. *Mark Wilson/Getty Images*

As Laura listens, President Bush reads the well-known poem "Twas the Night Before Christmas" to a group of students in the White House on December 10, 2001. The following year, after reading a page, he turned the book over to his wife, the former teacher and librarian, who was much better at commanding the attention of eager elementary school students. *Rich Lipski*/The Washington Post

On the day before her husband is sworn in as president, Laura Bush visits a fourth-grade class at Seaton Elementary School in Washington, D.C., and shares a hug with Louella Rawlings as Kellie Boler looks on. She is most comfortable and natural when visiting with students; dropping to a crouch to look directly into their eyes is second nature to her. *Rich Lipski*/The Washington Post

On a trip to Europe in May 2002 with her mother, Jenna Bush was so sensitive about being captured on film that she insisted a White House valet hold up her mother's garment bag to shield her from view. *Win McNamee/REUTERS*

With White House aide Israel Hernandez smiling at her, Jenna Bush watches her mother lay a wreath during a memorial ceremony in May 2002 at Theresienstadt [Terezin] outside Prague, where 140,000 Jews were processed for deportation to death camps. *AP/Wide World Photos*

Laura Bush takes a walk with her girls in Kennebunkport on June 12, 2003. She says one of the hardest parts of living in the White House is her distance from her daughters. "I hope they realize how much their mother misses them," she once said wistfully. *John Mottern/ Getty Images*

Jenna appears in court on May 17, 2001, in connection with her citation for possessing alcohol as a minor. She complained to the judge about photographers taking her picture through the courtroom door.
Peter Silva/ Zuma Press

A walk across the White House lawn: Spot leads the way, Laura holds her mother's hand, and the president follows, in June 2002. Jenna Welch is a frequent visitor to the White House, the ranch, and Camp David. Laura sometimes slips home to Midland and stays in the room she had in high school. *Hyungwon Kang/REUTERS*

President and Laura Bush at the Hermitage in St. Petersburg on May 25, 2002. The couple could spend all their time together, Laura's mother, Jenna, once said, and still be happy with each other. *Kevin Lamarque/REUTERS*

Looking a bit amused, Laura Bush graciously allows French President Jacques Chirac to kiss her hand on her trip to Paris, September 29, 2003. With that single image, carried on newspaper front pages around the world, the first lady was credited with improving, at least symbolically, relations between the United States and France, at odds over the war in Iraq. *Philippe Wojazer/REUTERS*

Laura Bush makes remarks at the gala dinner on the eve of her National Book Festival on October 4, 2003, which drew 75,000 lovers of literature to the Mall. Her signature event is also her favorite, igniting a level of passion obvious in her eyes. *AP/Wide World Photos*

the primary source of the first lady's power. The quality of her relationship with her husband has been the key factor in determining the extent of her influence."

The first time I interviewed Laura Bush, she remained deliberately disinterested in dealing with the question of herself as a symbol. For more than an hour in the Yellow Oval Room, on the second floor of the White House, we talked about her background, her interest in education, her marriage, her in-laws, her dogs. She was warm and readily amused, composed, and deeply calm. Laura wore a black knit pantsuit with a turquoise blouse and arranged herself on an ornate chair. She had a certain modesty to her, a quality that seemed almost quaint in an era of public egomania. Her hands looked strong and practical, gardener's hands, and she usually kept them folded in her lap. The nails were short and coated in light polish; she wore a simple wedding ring and small earrings. I remember being startled at the vivid color of her eyes; they were such a brilliant turquoise that I asked an aide later whether Laura wore tinted contact lenses. (She does not, I was told.) She laughed a lot, and her eyes laughed with her.

"It's a very odd job, there's no doubt," Laura said. She acknowledged that unlike the job of president, the to-do list of the first lady kept growing, "so you still have to preside over the Governors Dinner," she said, even if you were called upon to deliver a speech on reading readiness at a think tank earlier in the day. "You know what, the fact is, first ladies always had an intellectual part of the White House, not just the social part, and I think we don't give earlier first ladies as much credit as they deserve." And then she cited not her mother-in-law, one of the most popular first ladies, nor Hillary Clinton, whose impressive intellect always was front and center, but another Texas wife initially perceived as bland: Lady Bird Johnson. "Certainly, Lady Bird Johnson, who was one of my favorites, was very effective in the job," she said. "Actually, one of the blessings of being first lady is you have the chance to work on and focus on one or two major interests, and those interests are usually what the first lady was interested in and knew about. Like education for me. Or the use of native plants for Lady Bird. And in the end that makes such an impact that some presidents can't make, because their legacy is so much more mixed. They have to deal with every single issue. I think that first ladies who focus on a few issues can do well and be successful."

But then I asked her, "What do you think the American people's expectations are of you?" She displayed a hint of irritation. "I don't know that," she said shortly. "I don't have any idea." The corners of her mouth tightened just slightly. There was an awkward pause while I tried to formulate a response that might persuade her to expand, to share her thinking. Then she added: "I actually think that the American people think that the first lady ought to do whatever she wants to do." With that, she had made a subtle alteration to my question, which was not about what she would do, but about who she is. I wanted to explore how she thought people perceived her. This woman who carefully monitored the image that her husband presented to the nation—and whose instincts were dead-on in this area—refused to reveal any similar scrutiny of herself. She had drawn the curtain. She would not ruminate on that.

On that day, Laura had been first lady for just four weeks, and much of that time she had spent back in Crawford, making the Bushes' new ranch habitable for them. She certainly had some sense of the power of her position. "I also think that people expect and want the first lady to use whatever expertise they have to help America," she added, shifting once again to discuss people's expectations of the position, rather than of her specifically. "I mean, it's a huge platform. I'm very fortunate to have such an opportunity to work on issues that I venerate. I love houses. I like furniture. It's fun for me. I have a good time walking up and down these halls, I like that. At the same time, I like to work on other issues, outside the social realm."

Laura would struggle throughout her first years in office to fully absorb and exploit the influence her position gave her. Even after she had walked hundreds of times into rooms where people cheered, she would look over her shoulder involuntarily, to see who they might really be applauding. "Does she ever get used to that, how enthusiastic people are about her?" I once asked her press secretary, Noelia Rodriguez. "No," she answered. "I would have to say she doesn't."

In an interview about the first hundred days of the Bush administration, Mrs. Bush told CNN's Larry King, "I don't know why this surprises me, I should have known this, but I'm also thrilled with the forum that I have to talk about issues that are important to me. And I'm just amazed, really, that I have this opportunity, because my husband is president. I guess I knew it, but I guess I didn't really realize the full impact of it."

On the day before her husband was sworn in as the forty-third president of the United States, Laura Bush had her own debut at DAR Constitution Hall in Washington. The event, hastily arranged during the compressed transition period, was modeled after Laura's initial public offering as first lady of Texas. It was called "Laura Bush Salutes America's Authors," an acceptably vanilla title, and it had the feel of a gathering at a regional public library. It was a peculiar, unsophisticated affair, in a town where political events are perfected as art form, all precision timing and careful backdrop. The Bush administration would come to master the public appearance for maximum effect, but in those first frantic days, the communications staff had not yet grown expert at crafting for the cameras. And those who were capable of the grand moment were focused on the president, not his wife. Laura Bush already had made a few firm decisions, however. "First lady" was an honorific she spurned at every opportunity. She hated the title. From that very first day, her staff of seventeen was instructed to answer the phone as "Mrs. Bush's Office" and sign her correspondence "Laura Bush." And, if the message of her maiden literary celebration seemed muddled, Laura made clear she would aggressively tend her own image; there was something about one newspaper account that bothered her, and she demanded and received a published correction.

DAR Constitution Hall is the city's largest concert venue, near the White House, next to the national headquarters of the Red Cross and the Corcoran Gallery of Art. To many Washingtonians and those beyond, it forever will be known for its owners' disgrace in 1939, when the haughty Daughters of the American Revolution refused to let the great contralto Marian Anderson sing there because she was black. There is no mention of that on the hall's official history, of course. Instead, the Daughters have taken pains to point out that among those distinguished American entertainers who have graced the stage are Eddie Murphy and Whitney Houston, hosting HBO specials; the official history also notes that the Country Music Awards and *Jeopardy!* have aired from the hall. The message is implicitly unmistakable: That nasty business with Marian Anderson is way in the past, and now, we can be as low-brow and downtown as we need to be! Or as downtown as any organization can be whose membership requirements begin with "first you must establish your lineage." (Having established theirs, Laura and her mother were inducted into the DAR in May of 2001.)

On the morning of Laura's coming-out party, which was free and supposed to be open to the public, the 3,702-seat hall was only about half full. The tickets had all been distributed to Bush supporters, but many of them never showed up. Milling about ahead of time were a handful of the unconnected curious, the history buffs, and the Texas friends. The district attorney of Dallas and his wife were there, personal friends of Laura's from her time in that city. A lady in a good suit air-kissed another lady in a good suit, and her words floated up toward the proscenium arch: "The Argentinians called and said, 'Chase, why don't *you* be the ambassador!' " There were lots of people in fur, and lots of people in cowboy hats, and at least one woman in a fur cowboy hat. *New York Times* writer Elaine Sciolino approached a woman in a full-length lynx coat, who said her husband had worked with the campaign in Atlanta. Elaine asked her if she was afraid of protesters splashing her coat with paint. "No," the woman replied. "I have another one like it at home." Washington reporters sought out colleagues from Texas, who had come to town to cover the weekend's events, and asked them to please point out anybody who was important. Being big in Texas doesn't mean much inside the Beltway. In the front rows sat former President Bush and Barbara Bush and their daughter, Doro Koch Bush, with Jenna Welch. With her grandmothers was one of the twins, Barbara, a freshman English major at Yale University. Vice President Dick Cheney was there, along with his wife, Lynne, an author herself. Laura introduced her before him. Her second-grade teacher, Charlene Gnagy, also was sitting in the front row, and when Laura pointed her out as inspiration for her teaching career, the audience as one said "Awwww."

The salute began with filmed encomiums to this new first lady, so sharply different from the one about to vacate the White House, Hillary Rodham Clinton. Of her daughter, Jenna Welch said, "She was the most beautiful little thing I've ever seen," adding that the young Laura had refused to go to sleep without a story, "and begged for more than one." Bar said that "Laura sort of took charge in her own gentle, quiet way" after George W. was elected governor in Texas. "She knew immediately what to do and how to do it." The former president called his daughter-in-law "Laura Steady-As-She-Goes," and then added, "She is—I don't know if you want to say perfect, nobody's perfect—but she'll be an outstanding first lady."

After all that, the president-elect took the stage and introduced his wife with words he would come to use over and over again: "Her love for books is real. Her love for children is real. And my love for her is real." The audience leapt to its feet and applauded wildly.

Then Laura herself, wearing a garnet wool dress, stepped to the dais and gave some prepared remarks about the power of writing, mentioning *Uncle Tom's Cabin* and how Harriet Beecher Stowe's novel of slavery had moved the nation to civil war. She joked that her gathering was a librarian's dream: "Not only do we get to hear from five respected American authors but also, if anybody in the audience starts to get rowdy, I get to tell them to hush up." Her audience chuckled. Five authors, seated onstage, would read from their works, she said.

Then she settled into a chair onstage, hands folded on her lap, legs crossed in ladylike fashion, and turned her face expectantly toward the authors, like a teacher watching a prized student ready to recite. The authors were a fascinating combination. I couldn't figure out what their selection said about Laura Bush, or about America. There was historian Stephen Ambrose, who gallantly kissed the first lady's hand as he rose to read, and the cantankerous jazz critic and essayist Stanley Crouch. Her friend Stephen Harrigan was there, presumably representing Texas literature; his *The Gates of the Alamo* was critically acclaimed. Most surprising of all, given Laura's appetite for reading challenging literary fiction by provocative female writers, were the two women suspense writers onstage: Mary Higgins Clark and her daughter, Carol. I wrote in my notebook, "of all the female authors, why?????"

They were an unusual quintet of authors to celebrate; in a review of the event, *San Francisco Chronicle* book editor David Kipen called Ambrose "our leading chronicler of what white male imperialists have actually done right" and Crouch "our foremost critic of what black activists get wrong." But Laura loved reading mysteries to relax, and she introduced the mother-and-daughter duo as specializing in creating "people who are going about their lives, not looking for trouble, who are suddenly plunged into menacing situations." She paused, then added wryly: "I can identify with that." She was almost certainly referring to winding up in the White House, although anyone who knew about the fatal accident could not have helped but draw a parallel to that tragedy as well.

In the end, Laura had chosen authors who represented a diversity of gender and color, but mostly, she picked authors she liked. She was a catholic reader, an omnivore of literature; no book was a bad book if it got somebody reading, and only snobs could argue with that. Laura didn't like seeing herself misquoted in a newspaper account the next day, though. The story said she had joked that she could tell the audience to "shut up." As if such words would ever leave her mouth! Or any librarian's! A White House aide called the newspaper, and the correction was promptly printed, to make clear that America's new first lady used only the gentlest of words—hush up—to exercise control.

As I watched Laura Bush in those first months moving through her public events, I noticed how much more animated and commanding she was when acting solo. When she traveled with the president, she faded to background. It made me wince to see her do it, I have to admit, and plenty of other observers had the same reaction. As I watched her, George's earlier words were often in the back of my head: *"I have the best wife for the line of work that I'm in. She doesn't try to steal the limelight."*

One day several weeks after the inauguration, the education president and his educator wife took a swing through poor schools in downbeat chunks of the Midwest. Fulfilling a campaign promise, the Bush administration had decided to make education reform its very first initiative. The prioritization of "No Child Left Behind," the name of the sweeping legislation that would be introduced, was certainly political calculation, sanctioned by strategist Karl Rove. But President Bush also sincerely believed in everything his wife had told him, with passion, over the years: If children were not reading by third grade, they were lost, forever; that every child could learn to read, and excel, and perform; that methods of education had to be backed up by rigorous research, rather than implemented willy-nilly from anecdotal experience; that teachers needed better training. In those early months of the administration, there were high hopes and bipartisan cooperation for the reforms. Even wary Democrats began grudgingly to acknowledge that these new Republicans were actually serious about remaking education. In Laura Bush, the party that once argued for dismantling the Education Department and inveighed against teacher laziness now had a high-profile cheerleader who began each speech with words of thanks for all those who toiled at the front of the classroom.

The first stop on the Midwest tour was Columbus, Ohio, and Sullivant Elementary School, a tired, squat building of painted cinder block that crouched on the bad side of town, next to a minor league baseball stadium, a quarry, and a trailer park. Most of the students at Sullivant lived below the poverty line and didn't always show up for school. Families moved away suddenly. It was just the kind of school that Laura recognized instantly, as it shared many of the same characteristics with Dawson Elementary, where she had been librarian during the 1970s in Austin. Waiting for the event, which was to feature a roundtable discussion and a few classroom visits, I browsed the school library, a dismal place, dark and dusty and wholly uninviting. I had spent some years covering education in Philadelphia, and I had seen my share of schools with inadequate resources, but the Sullivant resource center was shocking. There were only three grimy, out-of-date computers. The library shelves held a bound set of *World Books*, the 1974 edition. Any child seeking to do a history report would have to rely on a tattered copy of the *United States Encyclopedia of History,* published in 1967, before the assassination of Martin Luther King, Jr., Watergate, the fall of Saigon. Nearby were neat boxes of crayons, both the classic colors and new, multicultural markers, designed to match a variety of skin tones.

The roundtable discussion began. The president talked, for ten minutes. He spoke about how the new emphasis on testing was not intended to be punitive but diagnostic. He talked about accountability. His wife nodded often. He repeatedly pronounced "children" as "chillun." She did not nod at that. The first lady displayed her uncanny ability for sitting very still. She did not speak. The superintendent of schools spoke, and the congressman for the region, and a reading resource teacher, who questioned the president on the White House plan to gather testing data and assess a school's weaknesses and strengths. She wanted assurances that someone in Washington would not deny funds without taking into account how hard it was to teach students like those at Sullivant, children who never had breakfast, came to school without supplies, children who grew up in homes with 167 channels of cable and not a single book, with a floating parade of surrogate parents but no known father. Laura listened intently. And then the parent at the roundtable posed a specific question, directly to the first lady. Her first-grade son had been diagnosed as learning-disabled, and she knew she had to be involved in advocating for him in the classroom. He was making progress, but he was struggling with writing. "Can you recommend any programs to write books as well as to read them?" the mother asked. "This is for you, too, Mrs. Bush."

Laura leaned forward and opened her mouth to answer—she still received and read her *School Library Journal* each month, and in her memory she had filed an exhaustive amount of research on what methodology worked and what didn't—but the president started speaking. "You should talk to your principal," he advised, vaguely, which was a particularly unhelpful answer, since the parent had the opportunity to get information from her principal every school day of the week. That mother was looking for the expert opinion. But as her husband gave his response, Laura immediately sat back into her chair and composed her face into that dutiful smile.

Then the visit to Sullivant was over, and the motorcade swiftly departed, past a handful of protesters. One held a sign that said, "Are George Reading?"

The second stop that day was Moline Elementary School in St. Louis, where a sign on the wall outlined the school rules: "Do not push, hit, throw objects or use gang signs." When the Bushes walked into a classroom, where twenty-four scrubbed third-graders sat, Laura gave her uniformly informal greeting, "Hi, everybody." "Good morning," they chorused, in that singsong way that children have. Billy Lyon read from "Amazing Grace," about a girl who learns, through reading, that she can be anything. Billy read with great expression, and Laura followed along with her eyes on the text, looking up from time to time to smile her approval at all the other kids. This was the real Laura whom George wanted folks to know. This was what she really liked to do.

The children peppered the visitors with questions: Do you ride in a limo? Do you ever get bored of your job? Do you have guards? Bush answered them all. Laura never spoke before he did. What's it like to be first lady? one of the children asked. "It's a lot of fun really. I get to live in the beautiful White House," she said, and I was struck, later, how much her language remained the same whether she was talking to children or adults. When I asked her how she was finding her life as first lady, she said, "It's exciting. It's really fun." Here again was her abiding characteristic: When discussing education, she was eloquent. When discussing herself, she reverted to reading primer syntax.

"What's your favorite story?" one of the children asked the president. "I like reading the Bible," he said. "There's a lot of good stories in that. And *The Willie Mays Story*." None of the third-graders asked Laura what her favorite book was. Since she talked to children the same way she talked to adults, would she have told them that her favorite story was a dark, difficult tale of human suffering and betrayal and loss of faith, *The Brothers Karamazov*? Now, that would have been interesting to hear.

A few minutes later, Bush rolled out his speech, intended to make news. He revealed a plan to spend $5 billion for reading over five years. After the applause, he waded into the audience, glad-handing the big shots, grinning widely and posing as thrilled school staffers handed their disposable cameras over to colleagues for a snapshot with the president. Missouri Governor Bob Holden got a big hug, and his press secretary, watching the scene, whispered to me, "I wish Mrs. Bush would talk more."

"She's pretty," said a school worker. "She is pretty," said another. But Laura was gone. She had slipped away into a classroom, where she knelt down and greeted each child, murmuring quietly to each one, stroking their arms and patting their hair.

The principal at Moline, Sarah Riss, had achieved success with an accelerated reading program, using a $75,000 grant to purchase materials. Her problem, she said, was getting good teachers. The best ones were those who had abandoned an earlier career that felt unfulfilling. Today's high school graduates, Riss said, went to college to find a career more lucrative than teaching. Money. Laura Bush could talk until she was blue in the face, advocating for early reading programs, congratulating teachers on the vital role they played in countless children's lives, urging retired military personnel to enter the classroom, but unless teacher salaries improved, reform efforts were going to fail.

Adele Acosta was principal at a poor school in suburban Maryland, where Laura chose to deliver her first solo address on her efforts. Acosta said money was her biggest barrier in attracting quality teachers to a school where many students were speaking English as their second language. "All my teachers have second jobs," she said. The salary was certainly an obstacle to recruiting, Laura readily admitted. "I'm sure that's why a lot of people don't choose teaching as a career," she told me, "and I'm sure that's why a lot of men never choose teaching as a career. In our country, it's mostly women." But for all her focus on the teacher shortage, Laura would not put word one in a speech about raising salaries for the nation's educators. "She will not single that out as a message point," press secretary Rodriguez said, "but clearly, Mrs. Bush believes that teachers are not as recognized for the work that they deliver and the impact they have on the future." Laura's reluctance to be more outspoken on the subject disappointed many of those education advocates who had been so cheered by her obviously sincere interest. "Where we part company with the first lady is in the idea that Troops to Teachers and Teach for America are the answer to America's teacher shortage," said Bob Chase, then president of the 2.6-million-member National Education Assocation, the country's largest teachers' union. Almost half of young teachers leave the profession in five years, he said, lured by higher pay and prestige elsewhere. "Solving the teacher shortage means solving the problems: low pay, insufficient mentoring, and professional development."

At César Chávez Elementary, Acosta's school in Hyattsville, Laura made it clear at the outset that those eager for her to lead the charge for better education were looking at the wrong woman. She would follow her husband on education policy. "I am proud to be part of President Bush's effort," she said, "to leave no child behind." Laura took great care to showcase herself as informed supporter, not policy advocate. In those first months of high hopes, President Bush had proposed increasing federal education spending by 11 percent, giving the Education Department the biggest hike of any cabinet agency. When his education secretary, Rod Paige, stood before the educators and media, he called the proposed $5 billion for early reading "staggering," then noted to Laura, "I know that comes from a little encouragement on your part." She smiled only slightly. Paige clearly hadn't gotten the memo: Never ever let on that the first lady is urging policy and spending on her husband. And when I later asked Rodriguez about Paige's remark, she said that Laura "hasn't worked on anything really formally. She is close to the president, of course, and education is near and dear to her heart, and that is all I am going to say." It was a very telling finesse. The beauty of Rodriguez's explanation was that it hinted at Mrs. Bush's expertise and gravitas and influence with the president, without overtly stating it, which might suggest she was secretly running the Education Department. The clear implication initially heartened liberals suspicious of Republican efforts toward education reform. "She can set a moral tone to get corporations to support some of these programs with money," said Peggy Cooper Cafritz, president of the school board for the dysfunctional public schools in D.C. "That her choice is so closely aligned with his priority is very important, because I think some of the best-laid plans are pillow talk."

"Mrs. Bush discovered the power of her office allowed her to do good and fulfill some of her career goals," said Margaret LaMontagne Spellings, Bush's domestic policy adviser. "We've seen a true ramping up in her engagement and comfort with being an advocate. But she never goes into enemy territory."

By July, six months into the presidency, Laura Bush had her signature style down. She hinted at everything but declared nothing. She had conquered feminism, according to the *New Republic*. Noting all the requirements of the role—"polished but not slick, accessible but not intimate, smart but not ambitious, beautiful but uncaring about her appearance"—Sarah Wildman declared that Laura "resolves this conundrum by filling all these contradictory expectations simultaneously. Or, more accurately, by allowing them to fill her. . . . She is the Play-Doh first lady: Mold her into whatever shape you want, then stamp her back down into a pile of putty for her next audience. Is it a pleasant existence? Probably not. It's certainly not an honest one. But for a public figure absurdly caught between society's conflicting notions of what women should be, it's a way to survive."

And while this analysis smacked of the truth, it also imputed to Laura Bush a level of shrewd calculation she did not possess. Her plasticity was not deliberate. If she accomplished a desirable level of malleability as political spouse, this was organic, not strategically and minutely planned. She acted the way she always had acted. Laura was clear about what she wanted to accomplish: "Right now, because my husband is president, I have this opportunity to talk about things that are important, and of course, as a former public school teacher, I think education is the most important," she told me in July of 2001 at Georgetown University, before she gave opening remarks at an ambitious two-day summit on early education that she and her East Wing staff had put together. "Look, Laura can set her own policy," President Bush said. "She's doing her own thing. And she's going to make a difference in people's lives. There's not this kind of coordinated campaign where she and I are at the top of our respective organizations and we sit down and plot strategy."

During much of the first half of that first year, Laura had spent her time immersed in domestic details. She had picked out pretty fabrics to redo her daughters' rooms in the White House, in hopes that if she made the rooms inviting enough the girls, away at college, might deign to visit. She hosted the ladies of her garden club during the Cherry Blossom Festival, inviting the press along on a garden tour. She had worn white gloves to meet the queen of Spain. Her long absences from the White House, during which she nested in the Bushes' new home at their Crawford, Texas, ranch, caused some raised eyebrows around the capital city. Hillary Clinton, by the end of her first six months, had plunged into remaking national health care.

Yet all the while, Laura, in her typically quiet way, without drawing any attention to her efforts, had been planning the early childhood summit. It paired experts in cognitive development with 450 government, business, and education leaders, so that they would have the latest research available to inform their thinking and decision making. Speakers included the cabinet secretaries for both education and health and human services, Rod Paige and Tommy Thompson, as well as Lynne Cheney, the wife of the vice president, and Senator Edward Kennedy, along with developmental pediatricians, Head Start directors, and brain researchers. Unlike the president's stump speeches on education, which were heavy on slogans like "reading is the new civil right" and "challenging the soft bigotry of low expectations," Laura's summit was dense with wonkspeak about "reading pedagogy" and "explicit phonics" and brain research. For two days, the first lady sat attentively down in the front row of the audience, listening to speaker after speaker, and never said a word. "It's a strange way to host a conference," said Wildman in the *New Republic*.

The summit format was constrained by the personality of the woman who hosted it, certainly. But it wasn't strange for Laura. I remember sitting at that conference and also finding Laura's presence particularly passive; now, I recognize that's just how she is. She learns by listening quietly. Rather than engaging others in a back-and-forth discussion, she needs a period of introspection to think through what she has heard. On top of that, she simply doesn't possess the dynamism to electrify a gathering, nor does she have any interest in doing so. And, as she did with her husband over and over again, she refuses to take any credit for what she might have accomplished by spending her personal capital as first lady. This is as startling as it is refreshing, in Washington, a city where people fall over each other to take credit for things they didn't do. But it also diminishes her effectiveness. Quiet isn't sexy in a quick-cut, sound-bite, twenty-four-hour-news-cycle political culture. That's not fair, but it's reality. As photogenic as Laura is, as polished as she has become in speeches and interviews, she really doesn't like the publicity. She just doesn't want the attention.

That day at Georgetown, I pressed her on her impact. "If you had a boss," I said, "would you have passed your six-month probation?" She just laughed. Rodriguez had to prompt her to talk up tangible results that Laura's bully pulpit talking had produced. Even then, Laura couldn't bring herself to brag. Rodriguez finally had to list her accomplishments for her: At least four thousand people had contacted Troops to Teachers since Laura had taken up the cause to enlist retired military as educators. And, after the first lady had appeared with Washington, D.C., mayor Tony Williams to talk up a program that trained second-career teachers, about one thousand people had applied for one hundred available positions. "That feels good," Laura said. Then she added: "I don't think I could take all the credit."

If this self-effacing nature limited her impact on issues, it did not diminish her public appeal; in fact, it only enhanced it. I asked her what had most surprised her during her first six months in office. Laura said she had been stunned at the scene she made in Italy, when she had toured the Leaning Tower of Pisa. Paparazzi had appeared seemingly out of nowhere, and tourists had surged around her, calling her name. "It was rather shocking," Laura said. "There were huge crowds lined up, and their response was just funny— calling 'Mrs. Bush! Mrs. Bush!' and clapping."

"Maybe you're just a magnet for Italian men," I said. "Obviously!" she said, and she chuckled and rolled her eyes. And there was the realness her husband was talking about, the kind he said Americans were starved for.

So she hated the idea of a role: "I'm not wild about the word 'role,'" she told Larry King on CNN. Laura's real job in the White House was her husband. He was her work. She would champion education and literacy to help her husband and the country, she said. "But I think I can help him also by allowing both of us to have a private life, to get away to our ranch, to entertain friends and family members at our ranch, which gives both of us the chance to relax and visit with people."

That explained why she took off two weeks after the inauguration. The construction of their modest home at their Crawford ranch had run over, as such jobs often do, and the Bushes had never properly moved in. "She wants to get the kitchen in order, the books in order," said Regan Gammon. "She wants to get it all in there and get it right and then not think about it again. She's a cleaner. She's just always been that way." Regan had teased Laura as soon as the election was finally called in December: " 'Boy, are you going to be busy. You've got a *really* big house to clean.' She just died laughing."

Her initial duties fulfilled, Laura left Washington and flew to Austin. She and Regan prowled through funky stores in South Austin. "She needed to get a bunch of stuff, sheets and stuff," Regan said. "And we looked all over old furniture stores in town for a piece of furniture she needed for a certain spot. The poor Secret Service agents had to run all over the place after us. I told her, 'I'm sorry about them, but we can't let you become a prisoner.' "

The $1.2 million Crawford home is as unprepossessing as its mistress, the woman with the Cover Girl makeup and the few pieces of good jewelry. And, because the Bushes built it from the ground up, it yields a great understanding of Laura's style, and, more important, her substance. Environmentalists find nearly nothing to applaud in President Bush's policies, from clean water and air quality standards to logging permits to oil drilling expansion to the refusal to sign the Kyoto treaty. But his house is a model of complicated, expensive, state-of-the-art ecological correctness. Even those eco-terrorists, the Earth Liberation Front, would approve. The house is small, undemanding of the environment, and full of utility. That vision was all from Laura, the closet naturalist and conservationist. That house is her defining project.

The Bushes hired an assistant dean of the architecture school at the University of Texas, David Heymann, and tramped their 1,600 acres with him for several weekends. He would drive small stakes into the ground, and the three of them would stand there, imagining the view from each contemplated room. Only a girl from Midland could love a dusty ranch where temperatures soared over 100 degrees in the summer and rain rarely fell, where the nearest town was Waco. The property is "very lonely, very severe. The land just rolls away, and you're just looking at nothing," Heymann said. Laura embraced the process of design and construction and took the details seriously. During the presidential campaign, as the couple crisscrossed the United States, Laura often sat poring over shelter magazines. Heymann said she was a fabulous client.

"Laura has a very, very clear emotional knowledge about her world and the way she wants it to be," he said, "and she uses that to make decisions. She wants you to feel about the house that while it is not demanding of you, it is also clearly intelligent." Just like her. What he learned about his client is that "she is so substantial that she is not insecure at all. She treats everyone the same way—very intelligent, very human, but she doesn't make a job of throwing it in your face. Her decisions are sensible and not strident."

Together, the architect and Laura created a house that is edgy and, at the same time, characteristically modest—only four thousand square feet, very long and narrow and integrated into the landscape. The walls are made of native Lueders limestone, not the creamy center of the stone that most builders find desirable, but the usually discarded outer edges, striped with color. A tin roof covers the home and its porches like a hat, so you can sit in a rocker outside without getting wet, listening to the rare rain beat a pattern of syncopation overhead. The house conserves energy by heating and cooling with groundwater deep beneath its foundation. A huge underground cistern collects wastewater, then recycles it to nourish the bluebonnets, native grasses, and honeysuckles that Laura planted. "It doesn't really look like anything anybody else has ever seen before," said Heymann. "It's a very interesting environmental machine that happens to be a very quiet building.

"Nothing screams to be noticed," Heymann said. "She cares a lot about design elements, and she has a very broad base of knowledge about a whole bunch of things—kitchen lighting fixtures, tile, door knobs. She was very concerned that the home be a place for living, not a flashy place, and when it came to choosing something, she would apply the same logic to that."

She was so engrossed by the construction process that Laura became interested in a group of meticulous carpenters. A small Christian collective founded by urban refugees that included many expatriates of New York, they had established an agrarian community near Waco. She learned all about them. Then she went to visit them and talked about their philosophy. Then she hired them.

She furnished the home simply and cleanly, painting the walls cream as a backdrop for original art by native Texans. She covered two new large sofas with a silky camel-colored cotton and mixed them with furniture the couple had owned for years, including a desk that had belonged to the first President Bush, and another one that had belonged to George's grandfather.

"It is a haven for us," she said, where we "want to grow old."

Heymann told me a particularly revealing story about how the mysterious mind of Laura Bush works: "In the powder room, there is no mirror above the sink. There is a window instead. You probably wouldn't think about that right away. You might wash your hands three, four times before you wondered why there is a window instead of a mirror. And then you might figure out that there is a window because a hundred feet away, there is a spectacular hundred-year-old tree, framed by the window. And that's why the window is there. That was her decision.

"And that's just how she is. She is only revealed over time, and with some thought on your part."

The ranch, on Prairie Chapel Road, is where the president fires up his chain saw, which makes his agents flinch with worry, and trims bush. It is there where the first lady weeds around her grasses and indigenous flowers and hikes through canyons and past a shimmering pond. They throw open the drapes to the dawn, and see vistas they love from the north and west and hear nothing but birds and the wind rustling the trees. She needed to create that place for them; she was acutely aware of how physically restricted her life had become as she stared out the windows of her armored limousine. She worked to make sure it did not become emotionally restricted as well.

Frequently, she would call up one of the friends she made in Washington when the Bushes had lived there during forty-first's presidential campaign, and they would go antiquing in Georgetown. The shopkeepers along Wisconsin Avenue grew to know her well. Her decorator friend James Powell came up from Austin and helped her redo various spaces in the family quarters of the White House. Together, they prowled the vast warehouse where prior occupants' furniture was stored, and she hauled back some of Jackie Kennedy's old pieces. As always, Laura could betray a depth of historical knowledge about the White House and its appurtenances, but only if you really pushed. "She can tell you about every piece and the history behind it and the president who was there at the time," said Mary Margaret Farabee, Laura's colleague from the Texas Book Festival. "It's pretty remarkable, but it's never her showing off."

When I asked Laura how she kept herself centered now that she no longer had cupboards to Clorox, she laughed. "Exactly. I've given that up," she said.

"I walk on the lawn with the animals—the dogs and the cats. Yesterday, I was riding back from visiting a friend that lives in Northwest [Washington]. We drove by that canal path along the Potomac. I looked down and there were a few walkers, and I thought, I can walk here. There were not that many people there. It was such a beautiful day. My garden club is coming," she continued, and she was looking forward to seeing Regan and Peggy Weiss. "They can go for great walks or runs early in the morning. I was feeling sort of envious that I couldn't go with them, so maybe I should walk on that canal path." It was a rare moment of her thinking aloud, trying to puzzle out what was possible for herself, and it gave a vivid example of everyday freedoms lost and sacrifices made by residents of 1600 Pennsylvania Avenue.

CHAPTER SEVEN

❧

The Twins

Jenna started crying and stated "Please" . . . She then stated that I do not have any idea what it is like to be a college student and not be able to do anything that other students get to do.

— Officer Clifford Rogers, in Austin police report

Early one mid-May morning in 2002, the reinforced black Lincoln Continental limousine glides silently to a stop several yards away from a U.S. military jet on the tarmac of Andrews Air Force Base. Laura Bush is about to embark on her first solo trip as first lady, a ten-day visit to three European nations, where she will speak out for Afghan women's rights.

An aide opens the door, and Laura carefully swings her legs out and steps onto the tarmac. At this point, she well knows her part: She pauses to give a smile and practiced wave, and Scott Applewhite, a veteran Associated Press photographer, dutifully records the image. The rest of us in her small traveling press corps know our part, too. We watch this routine preflight maneuver, and when the first lady goes up the stairs, we will turn from our spot behind the massive wing and troop up the back stairs to our part of the plane, well away from FLOTUS, the acronym for First Lady of the United States. But before we do, one worn corduroy leg swings off the limo's smooth leather seat, then the other. Jenna Bush stands up to follow her mother into the plane for this spring fling, and we reporters go on alert. It's the secret girl! The bad twin! The rowdy one, so defiant about being a first daughter that she has been busted twice for underage drinking in four weeks; has run her Secret Service detail ragged; has been photographed in the *National Enquirer* apparently falling down drunk, a cigarette in her hand.

Oh, Jenna.

The corduroy jeans have ratty hems, where Jenna has ground them into the pavement too many times. She is wearing flip-flops and a short black T-shirt, and her exposed tummy pooches out over the low-riding waistband. Her blond hair has been carelessly pinned up with a plastic clip. Sunglasses cover her eyes. Hoisting a backpack, she clomps up the plane stairs and disappears.

I think about my own college-age daughter, and how she would dress for a transcontinental flight. Better. "Oh, well," I think, "it's 7:30 in the morning, and Jenna probably just rolled out of bed, and she just got finished with school, where she probably slept in every day." After all, Jenna will have plenty of time to get herself together before the entourage lands in Paris, where French and American officials will stand at the plane's steps to greet Mrs. Bush and hand her flowers. The girl is hardly flying coach: Her mother has a hairdresser and a makeup artist on board the military plane, and there's a lovely wide bed and full shower.

But when we touch down at the airfield seven and a half hours later, and her ladylike mother smiles and embraces the waiting welcomers, Jenna appears at the plane door looking exactly the same. The flip-flops, the belly exposed, the hair still not brushed. Suddenly, she darts back inside. The twin has spied the telephoto lenses of several French photographers far away, behind a fence. For a few moments we wonder what is going on, and then the limousine trunk floats open by electronic remote. A White House valet has been asked to retrieve one of Laura's Neiman Marcus garment bags, carefully laid out in the trunk, and he carries it back up the plane's steps.

We watch in wonder. While he holds it aloft, Jenna slips behind it, and he walks back down the stairs, shielding the first daughter from the prying eyes of all press, foreign and domestic. Only the top of her blond head, bobbing up and down, and those damn thongs are visible. Jenna is hiding, literally, behind her mother's skirts.

It's the very beginning of ten days in the bubble of an official visit, with all that it implies: tight press controls, no independent reportorial forays, absolute insistence that queries about and coverage of the first daughter are completely off-limits. So there is no point in asking the question, "What's up with Jenna's appearance?" That way lies misery.

But there are only two possible explanations for what I have just witnessed. Either, a) Laura Bush has asked her twenty-year-old to please make herself more presentable, more fitting as a representative of the United States using taxpayer dollars on an official visit, and her daughter has adamantly refused, or b) Laura hasn't even bothered to ask.

There is plenty that the Bushes don't ask their daughters to do, that much is clear. Jenna and Barbara have not been asked to campaign. They have not been asked to rein in their adolescent rebellions. They have not been asked to appear even nominally interested in any of the pressing issues affecting this world their generation will inherit. They have not been asked to have any empathy toward the struggles and responsibilities facing their mother and their father, the president of the United States. Nor have they been asked to have respect for his sense of duty to others besides his own family. They have not been asked to treat with respect their Secret Service details, those highly trained men and women who literally would take a bullet for those girls. They have not been asked to show their faces at the White House very often. They have not been asked to make something of themselves in their own right, in the way that their father felt obligated to prove himself on his own, and his father did before him.

These girls have all the *noblesse,* and none of the *oblige.*

Since they were twelve and their father sought the governor's office in Texas, Jenna and Barbara have not been asked to think beyond "how much is my life gonna suck if this happens?" They are rich girls, blessed with intelligence, good looks, trust funds, loving parents, boundless opportunities, freedom from many of life's daily vexing challenges, yet they persist in seeing themselves as victims. In this, they have been subtly encouraged by their mother. Laura would never permit herself to feel victimized by George's decisions; she regards herself as a full partner who embraced his ambitions because she wanted for him what he wanted for himself. His happiness has been as important to her as her own, or greater. No, any victimization she might have felt has all been transferred onto her girls. Once George sought political office, Laura's guiding principle in mothering became "they didn't really ask for this," as if Jenna and Barbara were forced into some disastrous, bumpy detour from the normal smooth path toward adulthood. Their struggles are her only regret.

"They just want to do like every other teenager does," Laura would say over and over during the first years of the Bush presidency. She was not shaking her head over the twins' citations for underage drinking, or the tabloid photos that showed Jenna carousing. She was defending her girls' right to behave like the wildest college girls out there, if that was what made them happy, or to walk around looking like grungy slobs. Her declaration was the dead opposite of what most parents of teenagers say, which is, of course, "I don't care what other kids do. You are not other kids." Jenna's appearance as she disembarked in Paris was emblematic of how Laura regarded her girls: She wouldn't make them look or act a certain way. It was just too much to ask.

Jenna's been the outrageous one all along, the second born, the blond one, who lured her fraternal twin, Barbara, into various escapades. Or, alternately, she's the one who just isn't clever enough to avoid being caught, while Barbara, with her brunette hair and more studious appearance, gets away with even more wild behavior. Jenna's like Daddy. Barbara's like Mom. So goes family lore.

It's fair to consider how Laura's girls are turning out. Laura Bush devoted much of her married life to motherhood, never returning to her career as teacher and librarian. By the time the twins were born in 1981, Laura was thirty-five. The couple hadn't been sure they would ever be able to have children of their own, and then Laura nearly lost the babies late in her pregnancy, so she and George felt doubly blessed. Their gratitude was so deep and persistent that, over time, it has turned into indulgence. Additionally, Laura was so traumatized by that car crash in which she killed Mike Douglas that she never wanted her daughters to live with that sort of anguish and guilt. She determined she would do everything she could to prevent her babies from that sort of sorrow. Trained as a teacher, presumably aware from her extensive reading that hardship can produce strength and growth, Laura nevertheless has shielded her girls. She acknowledged that the tragedy had made her "extra-protective" as a parent.

In many ways, Barbara and Jenna were excellent candidates to make a good transition to life as the children of a political figure. It was the family business, after all. Their father knew all the advantages and pitfalls of public life; he was the child of a president of the United States. Admittedly, George was eighteen when his father first served in Congress, and thirty-eight by the time his parents moved into the White House. George and Laura had extensive training for life in the fishbowl. When they made a decision that he would seek public office, they did so only after they had addressed their concerns about what it would mean for their family. "She was the last one to sign on, the most reluctant," George said of Laura. "Our girls were so little," she said. Yet the timing could not have been more propitious. When their father became governor, Jenna and Barbara were able to go to high school in the relatively close-knit, laid-back town of Austin. By the time their parents landed in the White House, they were away at college. They never had to live there.

For the little girls, who called their famous grandparents Gammy and Gampa, the political lifestyle seemed nothing but fun: lots of bands and balloons and fancy parties; hamburgers on Saturday in the wonderful Vice President's Mansion, with its huge wraparound porch and its expansive hills, perfect for rolling down; rides inside limousines and down the polished wood banisters of the historic White House. It had a movie theater, and a bowling alley, too. You could have anything you wanted to eat or drink. It was like room service, only the food was better!

But during George's campaign for governor of Texas, the twins had their first taste of how difficult it could be to hear barbs directed at your daddy. At a bat mitzvah for one of their friends at a sports club, where the televisions were on, the group of kids saw an ad for Bush's opponent, the incumbent governor, Ann Richards. The girls were uncomfortable, said Laura. They didn't know how to react. But their friends did: they all loudly booed. Later, when a George W. Bush ad aired, they all cheered. "That support made them feel good," Laura said. Then she added, "At that age, you're still embarrassed that your parents are anywhere to be noticed."

When the Bushes first moved from Dallas into the Governor's Mansion in Austin, Barbara and Jenna went to the private St. Andrew's School, and a glance at their mother's daily planner showed how hard she worked to integrate her life as a mother with her duties as first lady. The girls' volleyball games and Laura's cafeteria duty were interspersed with her speaking engagements and with nighttime dinners and receptions downstairs at the Governor's Mansion, while the twins hid out upstairs. Even as they traveled around the state, Laura insisted that at least she or George be home by four in the afternoon, to help with homework. The four of them ate dinner together most nights. "You'd see them at back-to-school night, just like all the other parents, sitting at the student desks in the classroom," said an Austinite whose kids were friends with the Bush girls. "It was no big deal. They were just part of the parent population."

Sometimes, despite this normal routine, the twins would complain that Laura didn't tell them what was going on, usually when they wanted her for something and she wasn't available, or when a guest arrived to stay overnight. And she would get exasperated, because she gave them a printed schedule every day. But she kept her annoyance mostly to herself. After all, *the girls hadn't asked for any of this.*

Now there was staff. Now there were no chores. Cooking, shopping, gardening, cleaning—all were taken care of. In the mornings and the afternoons, Texas Department of Public Safety troopers chauffeured the girls to and from school. The Bushes, always frugal, sold the Chrysler minivan that George had given Laura for Christmas just a few years before. She recognized she was being deprived of an excellent way to gather teenage intelligence. Being relieved of driving "is actually a wonderful luxury for someone who drove twenty car pools a week in Dallas," Laura said. "At the same time, you learn a lot about your kids when you have them captive in a car. So I miss that a little bit. Especially at this age, when they become more secretive. You find out a lot in the car pool that you don't when you're not driving one."

There were other adjustments to life above the store. "In the morning, I can hear the tour guides," Laura said. "Barbara was home sick one day. Her bedroom is on the back of the house where the tour stops out in the garden right under her window. And she heard the guide say, 'The Bushes have a dog named Spot and a cat named Cowboy. And they have another cat, but I don't know that cat's name.' Well, that was Barbara's cat," she said, and she laughed.

"Barbara said, 'Mother, they don't know India's name!' She really kind of wanted to yell out the window and tell them her cat's name."

In interviews during the Texas governor years, both Laura and George again and again referred to how embarrassing their children found them. Always, they seemed to think this was perfectly normal behavior for teenagers. George had a tendency to get hurt and expect more courtesy of them. Laura would soothe him and tell him to be more understanding. She was the teacher and the stay-at-home mother, so he deferred to her. The couple bent over backward to have sympathy for their girls' plight.

"There's no such thing as not being governor," Bush said. Every time he went to one of Jenna's volleyball games, the opposing team would ask for an autograph and picture. "Jenna's and Barbara's reaction, of course, was total humiliation," he said. Laura seemed resigned to being an object of ridicule for her girls; they made fun of her clothes, her shoes, her hair. "Mom," they would tell her, "your hair is so stiff it would stay put in a hurricane." George and Laura often went to watch the Austin High School baseball team play on fall afternoons. One of the girls had a boyfriend who played on it, and Laura said those fall afternoons were some of her most pleasant moments. But the girls never wanted to sit with their parents, folks around Austin said.

Rarely were the girls asked to come downstairs and say hello to dinner guests, and so they were deprived of practicing manners. "We've been very careful not to make them go to things or be in the limelight," Laura explained. "At this age, they don't even like to admit they have parents." Later, during the presidential campaign, Laura would return to this theme again. The twins were proud of their father, she said, "and they want him, of course, to do whatever he wants to do, but at the same time, they want the privacy that I think every senior in high school wants. You know, most seniors in high school don't want to even admit they have parents, you know, much less a parent who is a governor or a presidential candidate."

Partly out of respect for their privacy, mostly out of sensitivity toward their distaste for their dad's high profile, Laura also asked photographers not to take the twins' pictures. Requests for a family portrait to illustrate a magazine or newspaper story were routinely denied. "The girls would be totally humiliated having to do a photo," said Laura. "And I know this sounds strange, but I'm just not ready to have everybody know what they look like." She made the girls sound just as shy and retiring as she had been, yet they were not. Both girls had insisted on a bigger world after junior high at St. Andrew's. "They didn't so much raise the possibility of attending public high school," recalled Terral Smith, the gubernatorial aide whose office was next to Bush's, "as demand it. They marched in one day, together. Jenna did the talking. 'This is where we are going,' she told him, and that was the end of that."

Jenna came out of the womb an extrovert. She loved being the center of attention, and she had self-confidence to spare. Her choice of extracurricular activity was ironic, given the Bush family's deep mistrust and distaste for the media; Jenna worked on the school paper. And she could be somewhat of a klutz; her classmates voted her "most likely to trip on prom night." Barbara, always more studious and organized, made National Honor Society and was elected homecoming queen. Unlike her mother, she adored fashion, especially putting together surprising outfits from vintage shops. Her classmates voted her "most likely to appear on the cover of *Vogue*."

When they were turning sixteen, they each wanted a car, so they could move about as they pleased. Laura thought it was a good idea. George refused. "You can share one car," he said, "and learn to work together." It was one of his rare victories in an attempt to impose some limitations on his children. Mostly, the girls got whatever they wanted. Laura's philosophy of adolescent maturation seemed to be that parents became helpless to influence their children during the teen years.

"It is very natural for them at this age to want to spread their wings, and George and I are certainly aware of that," Laura said. "We are aware of how much less relevant we are in our children's lives each day as they grow up and want to be with their own friends and are starting to think about where they want to go to college and where they want to be when they move away."

At other times, the girls seemed to display an equanimity about their father's political life. One morning at breakfast, one of the twins asked her mother, "Are we in the paper today?" and then returned to eating. And Laura indicated that the self-absorption that so defines the teen years had some protective qualities for their girls. "They are very proud of their dad," she said. But, "just like every teenager, they are mainly concerned with what they're going to be doing this weekend."

As the family began to discuss whether George should run for president, the girls' position was adamant and unwavering: No. Both would be in college before the election. They would never have to live in the White House or attend school in Washington, as Chelsea Clinton had done from the age of twelve, but that calculus didn't move them. To Jenna and Barbara, it was clear that their glorious emancipation from the strictures of living at home would coincide exactly with the arrival of a Secret Service detail to their college dormitories. Their every move would be shadowed, their every date tailed. "The girls didn't want him to do it because it would ruin their lives," said *Texas Monthly*'s Paul Burka. "And that was why Laura really didn't want him to do it." Burka pressed Bush on the topic one day while the two were flying back from a function for Ohio Governor Bob Taft. As high-level Republican figures pushed Bush to pledge his candidacy, Jenna and Barbara and Laura were pushing back.

"You're going to run" for president, Burka told Bush.

"Well, no, I don't know," said the Texas governor.

Burka suggested that any company would love to have Bush as a chief executive officer; he could cash in for millions.

"I don't care about that," Bush said. "I could care less."

"Then you're going to run," said Burka.

"Why do you say that?" asked Bush.

"Because there is nothing as interesting out there," said Burka. He saw it as inevitable, and he related a story to Bush to illustrate how a process, once set in motion, continued to its foregone conclusion. In Burka's case, his wife wanted a new house, and he didn't want to move. So she had painted the one they were in, which led to a sale offer, "and the next thing you know we were out on the street," said Burka.

"Houses don't cry," Bush answered instantly. But girls did. "I knew what that meant," said Burka. "They wanted to be normal teenagers."

There was something else that concerned the Bushes. Back in 1988, George W. had asked an aide from his father's presidential campaign to research what happened to presidents' children. The forty-four-page report that Doug Wead prepared was at once heartbreaking and disturbing. Offspring, particularly sons, had a fatal attraction to risk, he learned. Later, he turned that report into a book about first families, and he concluded, "There is no more remarkable common denominator among American presidents than their early encounters with premature death." He found that twenty-six children of presidents died before the age of five, and dozens more before they reached their thirtieth birthday. Many more suffered from defeat and failure, the result of expectations placed upon them by an exacting and driven father who had risen to the highest position in the land. Wead concluded in his book that the stress of the presidency passed to the children. It flowed from the instant fame and constant attention, and from seeing parents' failures publicly vilified. Hearing insults about those you loved was particularly damaging. And finally, Wead noted "the complete lack of connection between doing and getting," between working toward a goal and having it bestowed without effort.

Laura and George developed a strategy to prevent some of those pathologies from taking root in their girls. They were heartened by the way the media had been protective of Clinton's only child, never reporting her comings and goings around Washington, allowing her space to make mistakes. "We felt like the press had given Chelsea Clinton the opportunity to have privacy, to have a private life," Laura said. And they were determined that they would not burden their girls with heavy expectations about their role as Bushes. As Laura saw it, George hadn't fully emerged from under the weight of that expectation until he was forty. She refused to have her girls feel similarly obligated. No, they would just reiterate to the twins that their goal was that the girls should be happy. The only lesson they wanted to impart to their children, Bush said during the presidential campaign, was "that I love you. I love you more than anything. And therefore, you should feel free to fail or succeed, and you can be anything you want in America."

There were other guidelines, of course, but they seemed to be vague pronouncements about making the right decisions as opposed to the wrong ones. George and Laura gave very few specifics, at least in public, about how to tell right from wrong. Friends, family, and staff were adamant about not discussing the twins, a rule that would remain rigidly in place throughout Bush's presidency.

George and Laura finally convinced the girls, and themselves, that the twins could have relatively normal lives during the election season and beyond. The girls would not campaign. "We've always assured them that they don't have to join us on any campaign event," Laura said, and the twins rarely did. They flew to New Hampshire for the primary there, but Laura's insistence over the years that her children not be photographed paid off: Nobody recognized Jenna and Barbara as they stood at the polls with their cousins, holding signs aloft for their father. "They got to campaign anonymously, and they really had fun doing that," said Laura.

A few months before the presidential election, Laura dropped off the campaign trail. She helped Jenna move in at the University of Texas in Austin, where Jenna's godmother, Regan Gammon, could serve as a surrogate mom. And she installed Barbara at Yale University, where her daughter became the fourth generation of Bushes to attend the Ivy League school. It was a profound transition for all three Bush women, and they struggled to establish new patterns of relating to one another. The twins had shared rooms and attended the same classes and bickered with and clung to each other for eighteen years. They were separated for the first time in their lives, just as they plunged into a stage of life that demanded self-reliance. Their mother, who had doted on them and smoothed out the rough spots of their lives, now stepped away. Abruptly, she became an empty nester. Her husband was locked in a desperate battle for the presidency. He, at least, had something to distract him.

The president was much more liable to hint at his irritation toward his daughters than his wife ever was. Responding to a comment during the campaign from NBC's Tim Russert that the girls thought "dad is not as cool as he thinks he is," George began, "I'm the disciplinarian." Then he stopped, and corrected himself: "Both of us are the disciplinarian, but when you tell a teenager 'no,' all of a sudden that kind of reduces your coolness. . . . It's an amazing experience. Raising teenagers has been a fascinating experience. We love them a lot. And the only thing we know to do is to tell them, 'we love you, so stop trying to make us not.'"

He could defuse household arguments with his goofy humor, which Laura said she deeply appreciated. "When we had tense moments at home" with the girls, she said, "he could usually be funny in a way that would defuse the nervousness and the tension and make everyone laugh." Other times, it seemed almost as if George's displeasure flared into a hostility he could not conceal. Always, Laura stepped in to mend wounded feelings.

On Christmas Day 2000, the last holiday the Bushes would celebrate before moving into the White House, the family had lunch together. They all were flying to Florida the next day, to spend a few days with former President Bush and Bar and Florida governor Jeb Bush and his family. The exhausting, extended post-election period was over; a truncated time frame for assembling the administration lay ahead. The Bush men all were looking forward to relaxing and fishing.

After lunch, Jenna got a stomachache. It intensified steadily through the afternoon, and finally in the early evening, Laura bundled her into the limousine and the Secret Service piled into their black cars. The motorcade raced over to St. David's Hospital, five minutes away. After blood tests confirmed their suspicions, doctors ordered Jenna taken to an operating room, where they put her under anesthesia and removed her appendix. Laura slept at the hospital that night on a pullout sofa next to her baby. George was not present for the surgery; Laura waited alone. He visited later that evening, then returned to the mansion.

The next day, he went on vacation to Florida just as he had planned. As he boarded the plane, reporters inquired about Jenna's condition. "Maybe she'll be able to join us in Florida," the president-elect said. "If not, she can clean her room." The reporters stared at him, stunned. "I couldn't believe it," one of those present later said. "First of all, I'm a father, and I cannot imagine a scenario in which my daughter would have major surgery and I would just leave on vacation. And then he just seemed so snarly about it, like he was pissed at her."

Laura's response, on the other hand, surprised no one who knew her well. "Basically what we have always been are mothers, and our children always come first," said Lynn Munn, Laura's longtime friend from Midland. "I would have been amazed had it been any other way."

When inauguration day arrived, Jenna and Barbara dressed to be noticed. Both wore trend-setting outfits by Texas-born designer Lela Rose, whose suits sold in stores for about $1,200. Barbara chose a black-and-white wool houndstooth sheath dress with a flared pink leather jacket. Jenna wore a camel cashmere checkerboard duster-coat over a matching skirt and coat of camel and ivory checks, with a mossy-green cashmere sweater featuring yellow and orange polka dots. They had intended to wear sexy stiletto-heeled Jimmy Choo slingbacks, but the cold rain that day forced them to change: Both girls wore sexy stiletto-heeled knee-high Jimmy Choo boots.

Despite their attention-seeking attire, the girls hung back at the inauguration, unsure of what to do. As the ceremony began, the family had all gathered in front of the Capitol. President and Hillary Rodham Clinton were there, as was the defeated candidate, Vice President Al Gore, and his wife, Tipper. Former President Bush and Barbara sat nearby. The collected statesmen formed a re-markable tableau, and both George Bushes were visibly moved by the solemnity and historic import of the occasion. When the mo-ment came for Supreme Court Chief Justice William Rehnquist to swear in the forty-third president of the United States, Bush rose to place his hand on the Bible, which Laura was holding. The twenty-year-old girls fidgeted toward the edge of their chairs, then stood up uncertainly. They had spent their lives around politics; they had been at this very spot twice before, when their grandfather took the oath of office as vice president and president. Yet they had no sense of how to behave. Finally, it fell to Clinton. Smiling encouragingly, he gave each of them a gentle nudge and gestured to them to move closer to their parents. So Jenna and Barbara stood there, the eyes of the world upon them, looking down at their toes, their shoulders slumped. Their grandmother, seated behind them, had seen enough. In one swift, practiced gesture, she reached forward to her grand-daughters, first one, then the other. She put her thumbs between their shoulder blades and pulled their shoulders back and down. The message was clear: "Stand up straight! Remember who you are! We are Bushes, and Bushes stand up straight."

That evening the girls looked as if they were having some fun at the parties and balls; Jenna was famously photographed laughing with surprise when her father gave her such a spin on the dance floor that the top of her strapless gown started to slip down her chest. But within a few days, the twins fled back to their campuses. They would not return to the White House for months. They re-fused to come for spring break. They did not come to Camp David for weekends.

Their mother was sad. "The hardest part for me is that the chil-dren don't think of Washington as home. I have tried to get them to come here for spring break—one of them has two weeks—but they don't want to come here," Laura said. Her usual discipline faltered, and a bit of melancholy crept into her voice. "I hope they realize how much their mother misses them."

Jenna and Barbara had made a splash in their overtly fashionable outfits and boots. They looked fun and unconventional and a bit daring. The mainstream press honored the administration's request not to pry into the girls' lives. Their respective campus newspapers primly refused to cover them. But the tabloids had become in-trigued. Jenna and Barbara, people quickly surmised, were not like the preceding first daughter. And frankly, Chelsea Clinton was a hard act to follow. In many ways, she appeared to be the perfect presidential child. Nobody was ever going to be as good as Chelsea, a top student at Sidwell Friends School who seemed just as brainy and engaged by world affairs as her parents. During her years in the White House, rather than fleeing political life, she had embraced it. She displayed tremendous curiosity. She called her father's secretary and asked for a ticket to his State of the Union address. When her mother embarked on a tour of the most disadvantaged spots in India and Africa, she decided to go along. As an only child, she lived in an adult world, where she listened to adult discussions and was encouraged to develop opinions, to speak her mind. She hung out in the East Wing when her mother wasn't available. "Somewhere along the way, whether she chose it or not, it was thrust upon Chelsea that she would be watched and observed, thus making herself a role model," recalled a Clinton administration aide who was fond of her. "She knew when she was in the spotlight, and she behaved gracefully." She had preternatural poise at official events, which she attended with some regularity, and when she floated into her first state dinner in a silver-blue sheath, she looked thrilled to be there.

Chelsea went to parties and drank and had boyfriends just like any other teenager—which is what Jenna and Barbara craved—but Chelsea had a gift for keeping her mishaps out of the public eye. She cultivated the protection and support of other adults in the White House, and she treated her Secret Service agents with respect. Accordingly, they were more inclined to protect her when she got herself in jams.

The twins, meanwhile, had no formal introduction in the new rules that governed their lives. Those new rules were: 1) Everybody's watching, and 2) You're using public funds. Jenna and Barbara seemed to have decided that their agents were their enemies—and their chaffeurs, bellhops, and valets.

It only took a month after their dad became president for Jenna to land in the headlines. It seemed that William Ashe Bridges, a young gentleman attending Texas Christian University in Fort Worth, had been at a noisy college party near campus, and had the misfortune not to vacate the premises before the police arrived. He was cited for possession of alcohol and public intoxication and spent four hours in jail. Around 6:00 A.M., a black Chevy Suburban with Virginia plates pulled up to the jail. Inside were Secret Service agents and a young woman. Bridges, who had gone to high school with Jenna and was "very vocal" in insisting he was her boyfriend, according to Tarrant County officials, had called her on her cell phone. Then he handed the phone to a sergeant, and Jenna asked when he could be released. "No one asked for any special favors whatsoever," said Sheriff Dee Anderson. The White House refused to comment about the incident, and so did the Secret Service when a spokesman was asked about the propriety of using agents to spring drunk kids from the county clink.

It was the first of many conundrums the Bushes would face as their daughters traversed their last years of being minors. Should they reveal the particulars of an incident to prove that nothing improper had happened, or maintain the adamant no-comment policy and allow questions to bloom into controversy? Bush opponents and many Democratic voters, still bitter from the election and the Clinton impeachment debacle, were hyper-alert for signs of hypocrisy. Now those critics wondered if the nation had replaced a womanizer with a teetotaling, law-and-order Bible quoter whose daughters were behaving as if they were in a *Girls Gone Wild* video. Within weeks, the *National Enquirer* had printed a full-page photo of Jenna apparently falling-down drunk, laughing and holding a cigarette, crashing to the floor atop a giggling female friend. Meanwhile, Barbara had given the slip to her Secret Service detail as she and some fellow Yale students drove to Manhattan to a World Wrestling Federation match, according to an article in the Yale magazine *Rumpus*. Using an electronic pass to go through a tollbooth, the car in which Barbara was riding then speeded up and left the agents, who were paying their toll in cash, behind. "They put on their sirens and sped 120 miles per hour until they caught up with us," the magazine quoted one passenger as saying. Yale officials ordered the staff to destroy copies of *Rumpus* and removed the story from the magazine's website, but not before the story had gained a wider circulation.

Laura was unable or unwilling to rein in her rebellious daughters. They vexed her and worried her. The twins seemed to be having trouble distinguishing between right and wrong decisions. Jenna and Barbara refused to consider how their behavior might reflect on their parents. And they were so self-involved that they failed to recognize that their mother, who now had a full-time job for the first time in their lives, might have other claims on her time. Laura's visit to Moline Elementary School in St. Louis came a few days after Jenna's detail had picked up her busted pal, but before the story had broken in the papers. When the third-graders in the classroom asked about her children, Laura said, with an unexpected bite in her voice, "One of them just called me on the phone and I guess she thought I would take care of her health problem from the school here?" The little kids blinked at her, uncomprehending. It was a mother's rhetorical question, unanswerable. The girls' father had the same problem. "Right before he's gonna make the State of the Union, after 9/11, he calls me up, exasperated, says, Jenna has lost the sticker for her car," said Robert McCleskey, who, as the Bushes' personal accountant, was dispatched to fix such problems.

Even when Laura was confronted with solid evidence that her girls were deliberately and dangerously evasive with their agents, she refused to correct them. The agents were told to back off. The press was blamed for the reports. It was always somebody else's fault. Even after Jenna was busted for underage drinking twice in four weeks, Laura's feeling was that her girls were just behaving like ordinary teenagers. The twins were just singled out for unfair attention because of who they were, she believed.

That first summer, Jenna sat in a crowded bar and tried to sweet-talk the bartender into breaking the law and serving her. The bartender was on the verge of capitulating—until he saw the guys with the earpieces nearby. He approached them and asked what to do. The agents shrugged. "Use your best judgment," they told him, and he promptly asked the daughter of the president of the United States to leave the premises. Jenna was furious. She bitched at her agents, then fled down a back alley. They gave chase, and when they caught up with her, she taunted them: "You know if anything happens to me, my dad would have your ass."

But when she called Daddy to complain that her detail was interfering with her drinking, he sided with her agents. Not so her mother. Laura didn't want her girls to feel constrained, and the agents were ordered to pull back from traditional methods of coverage, according to an account of the incident in *U.S. News & World Report*. The magazine article was a lengthy, serious investigation of problems facing the Secret Service, and the Jenna anecdote had been introduced to illustrate the agents' many concerns. But Laura was so angered by the story that she canceled a scheduled interview with the news magazine. The messenger got the blame.

"Agents are not baby-sitters, and we are not servants," said one who had served on Chelsea Clinton's detail. "Don't treat me like dirt. Chelsea would forget we were outside, by the curb, all night. We'd go to someone's house, and then she'd decide to sleep over, but she wouldn't tell us what was going on. So I would go right up on the porch and ring the doorbell at 2:00 A.M. and wake people up. 'Excuse me, miss, but are we here all night, or are we going home?' And then I would tell her, 'Don't leave us out here without a bathroom break or anything.' She got the point. You could work with her. You could make a relationship based on mutual trust and respect. These girls don't understand that."

Three months into the presidency, the girls landed on the police blotter, and now the mainstream media could not ignore them. In late April, after an Easter break spent at the Crawford ranch, Jenna and some friends left the University of Texas campus and headed for Austin's Sixth Street. The strip has more than a hundred bars, and on every night of the week, it pulses with thumping house music and stinks of beer and vomit. Like carnival barkers, men stand in the open doorways of the bars, complimenting girls in their teeny halters and micro-minis and talking up the night's specials. Jenna was fond of Cheers Shot Bar, a long, narrow, dark dive where the blackboard specials included plenty of get-trashed concoctions named for sex acts and body parts—Buttery Nipple, Red-Headed Slut, Screaming Orgasm. By 1:30 A.M., Jenna was sipping a beer when the cops came in. The nineteen-year-old got a ticket for underage drinking, joining the several hundred unlucky young people similarly ticketed in Austin each year. The citation provoked much editorializing about the need to lower the twenty-one-year-old drinking age. "The Bush girls, after all, are nineteen-year-old adults, old enough to vote or go to war or pilot a plane or run for Texas county sheriff," wrote Gail Collins in the *New York Times*. She noted that President Bush was "in a particularly weak position when it comes to issuing warnings about how too much partying can hamper your ability to find a good job in the future."

A few weeks later, Jenna appeared alone before Austin Community Court Judge Elisabeth Earle. Wearing a tight-fitting sleeveless black shirt, pink Capri pants, and sandals that exposed a toe ring, she pleaded no contest and was ordered to pay $51.25 in court costs, perform eight hours of community service, and attend a six-hour alcohol awareness course. During the brief appearance, she complained to the judge that photographers were trying to take her picture through windows in the courtroom doors, and the judge had security shoo them away. "Good luck to you, miss," Earle said, and that episode seemed over.

Until . . . Oops, they did it again! as *People* magazine screamed on its cover. Next, both twins were cited for underage drinking violations. Just two weeks after her sentencing, Jenna went with Barbara to Chuy's in Austin, a joint known for its Tex-Mex food and killer margaritas, where a sign over the bar reads "I'd Card My

Own Mother." This was a tough policy that paid off. According to the Texas Alcoholic Beverage Commission, the restaurant had never been charged with serving minors in its history, and all of its staff had attended all the recommended training courses.

The sisters and three friends slipped into a table at about ten at night, and the bartender immediately recognized the president's fair-haired daughter, according to the account he later gave police. He called over the table's waitress, Shannon Stewart. "The blonde in the pink halter top is Jenna Bush," he said. "You'd better card the whole group." When Jenna tried to use a Texas driver's license with a picture that didn't look anything like her, the waitress refused to serve her. "Whatever," Jenna said, and asked for some water and chips.

Stewart did serve the group three margaritas and three shots of tequila, according to the police report, which were drained. Restaurant manager Mia Lawrence called 911, an unusual move in a town where UT officials estimated that 90 percent of their 49,000 students drink. When police arrived, Lawrence told them: "I want to get them in big trouble." When Austin officer Clifford Rogers asked to see Jenna's identification, she burst into tears. "Please," she implored, according to the officer's account in the police report. "She then stated that I do not have any idea what it is like to be a college student and not be able to do anything that other students get to do." After an extensive two-day investigation, both twins were charged with misdemeanors. Jenna was booked with misrepresenting her age to buy booze, a charge complicated by the citation already on her record. She faced far stiffer penalties for the second offense, under Texas's tough "zero tolerance" policy, which her daddy had signed into law in 1997. Barbara was charged with being a minor in possession of alcohol. Barbara pleaded no contest and got the eight-hour community service and an order to attend alcohol awareness class. "You might say this is a pretty simple investigation, and a lot of times it is," said David Ball of the Texas Alcoholic Beverage Commission, "but this one has a high profile, and everybody has obtained an attorney."

Again the White House refused to comment. "If it involves the daughters and their private lives, it is a family matter," said spokesman Scott McClellan. This episode was egregious enough that it needed some spin, however. A senior administration official let slip to CNN that a "not happy" President Bush had called Jenna up from California, where he was talking up a park preservation program. There would be no word from Laura, however. Asked if she had spoken to her daughters, aide Ashleigh Adams said, "If she did, that would be private. Out of respect for the girls' privacy, we don't comment on them." In the days that followed, press secretary Ari Fleischer repeatedly lashed out at reporters who tried to ask questions about the incident.

The twins' grandmother Barbara drew roars of laughter when she suggested, in remarks to the Indianapolis Junior League, that President Bush was "getting back some of his own," referring to the troubles he had given her. But a few days later, at a literacy event in Maine, she scolded a television reporter who tried to ask about the girls' troubles. "I'm not going to discuss that, and I'm a little embarrassed for you that you asked."

Jenna and Barbara were summoned to Camp David for the weekend. It was the first time they had been there since their parents moved into the White House. George and Laura were there, as were Bar and former President Bush. The grandparents were upset with the twins, and with all the coverage. What emerged from that family intervention was the twins' renewed dedication to not get caught: Both girls managed to stay off the crime docket for underage drinking. When they finally turned twenty-one, White House aides breathed a huge sigh of relief, and more than a few privately toasted the twins. Mom threw the girls an elaborate party at the ranch, and busloads of revelers arrived dressed in costumes according to the theme, cowboys and Indians. The ever-sassy Jenna insisted on celebrating her actual twenty-first birthday, however, at the scene of her original crime, Cheers Shot Bar, where she had staff cover the windows with black paper to prevent news crews from seeing inside.

The twins, who Laura acknowledged "kind of give each other permission to misbehave," hardly seemed chastened. Instead, they ramped up their revelry. They still claimed that Daddy's choice of employment had ruined their life. In the spring of 2002, while on that European trip, Laura Bush was asked if her girls had gotten more used to the limelight. "No," she said, "I would have to say not. They're going to be juniors in college. They just want to do like other teenagers do." At the same time, those girls had become expert at exploiting the notoriety they had gained as the president's daughters. Neither Bush twin had to stand behind a velvet rope line. Jenna and Barbara glided into exclusive nightspots and celebrity-packed parties around the world.

After finishing her community service at an art museum, Jenna took off for Hollywood and an internship with the entertainment management agency Brillstein-Gray. One night, she and Barbara and a posse of twenty danced the night away at Deep, where staff tried to keep anybody under twenty-one out because of the club's R-rated shows. The Bush girls were special, acknowledged a staffer, "because they got the hookup with the big guy." In St. Tropez, Jenna partied with Sean Puffy Combs. In New York, the twins sent one of their agents out to procure an introduction to rocker Chris Cornell, the frontman for the band Audioslave. The girls were not averse to showing up at places where controlled substances were enjoyed. Barbara attended a Four Seasons Grill Room party for wunderkind designer Zac Posen, where the dancing was dirty and the air smelled of pot. In Los Angeles, they showed up at a Nike party, where they met movie star Ashton Kutcher, who ended up taking them back to his house. He told *Rolling Stone,* "So we're hanging out. The Bushes were underage-drinking at my house. When I checked outside, one of the Secret Service guys asked me if they'd be spending the night. I said no. And then I go upstairs to see another friend and I can smell the green wafting out under his door. I open the door, and there he is, smoking out the Bush twins on his hookah."

No comment. No comment, no comment, no comment, said the White House. The problem with such a communication strategy was that the only public image of the twins was a highly unflattering one. If they were feeding the homeless, or tutoring poor children, or writing impressive senior theses, no one would ever know. If she talked about her girls at all publicly, Laura was given to making bland, nonspecific declarations of love and support. President Bush was slightly more revealing. "I love them a lot. I am impatient with them. I wanted them to be normal when they were teenagers, and I wanted them to be working ladies," he said. "I've got to slow down. I've got to allow them to become the bright young ladies that they're becoming at their own pace, and not at mine." He would mention life's challenges, and Laura would talk about how her daughters amused her. "I think they're a lot of fun to be with," she said. "I guess I would say that I'm engaged by them, with their personalities. . . .

"I think, like every parent, if your children are happy, then parents are happy. And if they're unhappy, then there's nothing more difficult for parents."

As the girls headed toward their senior year in college, the Bushes indicated the twins were thinking about Teach for America, one of Laura's pet projects, a service corps that recruited recent college graduates who had not been education majors and dispatched them to struggling urban schools.

"They are beginning to realize that they've got to take some responsibility for their own lives and beginning to think about their career paths," their father said, hopefully. "Laura chose her career path . . . early. I didn't choose mine until a little late. And uh," the president said, chuckling, "I never really was that worried about the career path."

CHAPTER EIGHT

September 11

I believe I shall see the goodness of the Lord in the land of the living.

—Psalm 27

When the Bushes finally held their first state dinner there was such great anticipation that all sorts of unseemly wrangling went on for invitations. Unlike the Clintons, whose state dinner guest lists ballooned toward seven hundred, spilling into white tents on the lawn, Mrs. Bush decided to hold the dinner to honor Mexican president Vicente Fox in the State Dining Room, which only seats around 130. She wanted intimacy, so that her guests would depart feeling they had enjoyed real conversations. "I think it makes for a nicer evening," she said. After the traditional receiving line, the meal begun with Maryland crab and chorizo pozole, followed by bison crusted in pumpkin seeds, a fava bean and chanterelle ragout, and a salad of gold and red tomatoes. And longtime White House pastry chef Roland Mesnier created an elaborate mango and coconut ice cream dome, topped with fresh peaches and raspberries, served with a red chili pepper sauce and a tequila sabayon. Two of the wines came from California vineyards established by first-generation Mexican-Americans. Laura loved being involved in the planning of such menus; anytime you would ask her, she would make jokes about her cooking prowess, but in truth, her friends whispered, she was somewhat of a gourmand and knew far more about exotic ingredients than she let on.

It was a magical night, and Laura looked very happy. She had even chosen something flamboyant to wear. Her gown by Arnold Scaasi had a hot pink off-the-shoulder bodice covered in beaded red lace and a full red taffeta skirt. A massive rhinestone necklace adorned the décolletage she always took such care to hide. Clint Eastwood was a guest, as well as the great tenor Placido Domingo, whom Laura adores. After dinner, soprano Dawn Upshaw performed in the East Room, and then the guests were led to the balcony off the Blue Room. There, overlooking the Ellipse, the Bushes had a surprise for their 130 guests to end that lovely evening of September 5, 2001. The famed Zambelli fireworks company designed a gorgeous twenty-minute display of pyrotechnic virtuosity, sending up 769 booming, blazing shells that dazzled the party and resounded for miles.

Within seconds, 911 switchboards across the area lit up. Residents on both sides of the Potomac were frantic. They feared the nation's capital was under full-scale attack.

Laura Bush headed for Capitol Hill on the morning of September 11, 2001. Over the weekend, there had been another gala dinner, this one at the Library of Congress, to kick off her first National Book Festival. Laura had successfully transported her signature achievement from Texas to the National Mall. The day after the black-tie dinner, she invited everyone to "revel in the joy of the written word," and the free festival drew some 25,000, who moved among a marketplace of books and ideas and nearly sixty authors, from signings to readings by basketball players to visits with Clifford the Big Red Dog. The magnificent library building was open for self-guided tours, the long East Lawn was a theme park for bibliophiles, and Laura walked the grounds ecstatic at the festival's success.

"That week before had been really, in a lot of ways, the culmination of what I thought it would be like to be the wife of the president, to live in the White House," she said later, and there was a wistfulness to her voice.

Three days after the book festival, on Tuesday morning, she had breakfast with her in-laws, who had spent the night, and then walked them to the door of the White House to say good-bye. The elder Bushes were headed to Minnesota, where the former president was to deliver a speech. President Bush was already gone, headed to Florida for an education event in a Tampa classroom. She was about to go to work, too. The first lady put on a red suit, checked her purse to make sure she had her Altoids and some Kleenex, and went downstairs to her motorcade. In a show of respect and bipartisan comity, Senator Edward Kennedy, a Democrat, had invited Laura to testify on early learning fundamentals before the Senate Education Committee, which he chaired. As only the fourth first lady to testify before Congress, she thought she was about to make history. Instead, history was about to make her.

I got my kids off to school, hung my congressional press pass around my neck, and hopped on the Metro for the twenty-minute ride to Union Station, which was a short walk from the Russell Office Building, where Mrs. Bush was going to speak. The train was packed, with commuters standing in the aisles, but people seemed cheerful and full of purpose. Official Washington always gets a snap to its step after Labor Day. The interns go home, and the brisk Hill staffers return, swinging their briefcases and speaking in their earnest secret language of governmental acronyms. Everybody trooped out of the station and into the bright sunshine of September. The sky had that startling blue color it gets in fall, and the dome of the Capitol gleamed especially white that morning. I was preoccupied, worrying about how I could make another Laura Bush education story, my fourth, interesting for readers. My own workaday problems, in my own little world, just like the rest of us. I knew Mrs. Bush's appearance was significant, but I knew it would be staged and static, with the first lady reading from a prepared speech. Inside the Russell entrance, a couple of Capitol Hill policemen kept an eye on the metal detector and teased each other about the price of boutique cups of coffee. A regular morning. I glanced at my watch. Plenty of time. It was only five minutes after nine.

As I turned down a corridor toward the hearing room, the first lady's deputy press secretary, Alison Harden, came flying down the hall at me.

"Oh, thank God, there you are!" she said.

"Well, yes, you knew I was coming," I said, and I smiled at her. "I'm not late, am I? Where did you think I was?" Ali was twenty-three, a capable young woman from a small town in Indiana, who came to work every day in the White House with a sense of wonder and disbelief that she had landed a job in such a hallowed place.

"I just didn't know where you were!" she said, and she looked as if she was about to cry.

"Ali, what's the matter?" I asked her.

"A plane hit the World Trade Center it might be a little plane they think it might just be an accident!" she said, all in a rush, and she looked at me, as if she was hoping to be reassured.

I thought, but didn't say, "No, they've come back to finish the job."

Somebody else standing in the hall said, quietly, "Another one just hit the other tower." A group of us pressed into an empty conference room, where Senate aides were clustered around a television set. Reporters pulled out their cell phones and began calling their news desks. No one knew what was going to happen next, anywhere. The education committee meeting was first postponed, then canceled. The senators and Mrs. Bush would not be making any statements to the press, said Jim Manley, Kennedy's communications director. Then the senator decided they should. Everyone did their jobs, calmly. Nobody ran. There was a sense of alarm but not panic. I remember being impressed at the professionalism.

The first lady was sequestered in a room with Kennedy and Senators Jim Jeffords and Judd Gregg, waiting for news. Her Secret Service agent had whispered into her ear the news of the first plane, as she got into her car to travel to the Hill.

"I thought it was an accident or something," she told me later. "I didn't immediately think it was terrorism. And then by the time we got there, we knew the second plane had hit, and so we knew it was terrorism." Instinctively, she shifted into her mode of thinking of others and anticipating their needs. "Even after the first one, when I thought it was just an accident, I thought we probably should can-cel," she said, "because Mrs. Clinton was on the committee and she's from New York and she'd probably want to rush home at that time." Waiting to hear from her husband, who had been hustled out of his classroom visit and was now up in the skies in *Air Force One,* she thought about the irony of being beside Kennedy at such a tragic moment. What she called her generation's "day of infamy" had been November 22, 1963, when President John F. Kennedy was assassi-nated in Dallas, and she remembered sitting in her high school classroom "feeling as if a blanket had been thrown over our school, suffocating all the usual sounds of chair scrapings and classroom chatter. The horror was so sudden and unimaginable." As she waited with the senator, she had "a depth of feeling" she couldn't even voice, so the two of them talked about "really mundane things," the Capitol and its offices there, and their dogs. Kennedy's dog, Splash, had come to work with him that day, and the brown Portuguese water dog came and rested his head on her knee. For the only child from a dusty town in West Texas, who had grown up loving pets, "there was something very comforting about that," she said.

About 9:30 A.M., we reporters and cameramen were ushered into the ornate Russell Hearing Room, and the three senators and Mrs. Bush walked out to see us. As soon as I saw her, I knew right away that she already understood: Her golden life had changed forever, harshly, precipitously. We looked at each other across a red rope cor-

doning off the senator's seating, and I, the supposedly trained observer, had to fight an impulse to turn away. She seemed that vulnera-
ble. My heart lurched for her. She fought back tears, and she clenched
her fists by her side. She never had done that in public before. Later,
she explained. The tears were for the nation. The tears were for her
husband. Characteristically, she added, "I don't really worry about
myself." Deep down, she is made of steel; there is no doubt about that.
In those first moments, she stepped up. Resilience is embedded in the
American character, and it certainly is part of hers.

A grave Edward Kennedy made some defiant statements about
how the nation's vital work on education would continue. Then it
was the first lady's turn to speak. "Our hearts and prayers go out to
the victims of terrorism, and our support goes to the rescue workers," she said, haltingly. Then, as she and the senators turned to
leave, Larry McQuillan of *USA Today* called out to her: "Mrs. Bush,
what do you say to the children?"

She paused. "We need to reassure them that many people love
them and care for them," she said, softly, "and that while there are
some bad people in the world, there are many, many more good
people. We can turn off the television and we can spend time reading to our children." In that moment, answering the question, she
said later, she found a purpose.

The grim photo opportunity ended, I hurried to call the newspaper and file the quotes. As I moved closer to one of the building's
tall, beautiful leaded glass windows to get better cell phone recep-
tion, a Capitol police officer practically tackled me.

"Get away from the window!" she yelled.

"Why?" I asked.

"Because we're under attack!" she said. "There's still one plane
up there, and it's headed right for us!"

As I glanced out the window over my shoulder, I saw huge
clouds of thick smoke billowing up from the south, pitch black
against the vivid blue sky.

"What the hell is that?" I demanded.

"A plane's gone into the Pentagon," the officer said.

The day was chaos. "I have never been at such a level of fear in my life," said the first lady's speechwriter, Charlie Fern. "It was mayhem. It was Armageddon. No one was obeying traffic signs. It was gridlock. And you would look over your shoulder and see that black smoke in the sky and think, 'Oh my God, what if there are more planes?' We were trying to drive away, and I was looking at the Capitol, waiting for it to blow up. And do you know what was even worse? The next day, we all went back to work. . . . that's when the alarms went off."

Twice the next day, the White House was evacuated. Workers streamed out of the stately old building and the Eisenhower Executive Office Building next door, men running so fast their neckties blew over their shoulders, women carrying their pumps in their hands. "I think it changed the structure of my brain, it was so powerful," said Fern. "I mean, there you were, so many people who had gone there thinking they had this glamorous, wonderful, ideal job. And then suddenly realizing that any minute you could die."

Laura Bush seemed galvanized into action. The woman who had the capacity to lie for hours on a sofa, reading, was suddenly logging sixteen-hour days, and in full public view, perfectly groomed, suit pressed, hair in place, and always, waterproof mascara. She reached out to comfort those closest to her and, through the medium of television, those she would never meet. The same emotional clarity that had guided her in composing her life now informed a new mission. She got on the phone to Kathleene Card, the associate pastor of Trinity United Methodist Church in nearby McLean and the wife of White House chief of staff Andy Card, and asked her to please be available to her staff. "The youngest members of my staff wept a lot, that first day," said Laura. "They were sort of freaked, I guess. The next day, the older and more mature members would sort of fall apart, and the younger ones were comforting them. We had a staff meeting the next day, and I said, 'When you sign on to work at the White House, you accept a lot of risk, and you know you can anticipate some things that may be bad and tragic, but none of us expected this.' "

But at the same time, she told them, "We are in a very special place. It gave us a chance to actually do something, to be constructive, to figure out what would be helpful, what my whole staff and I could do to help the situation. And one thing being able to help does, it relieves those feelings of helplessness. And that's true for everybody," she said. "For children making cards. All those people who stood in line to give blood, that's why they stood there, because they literally were going to give a part of themselves to try to help their fellow Americans."

The day after the attacks, Laura visited the Pentagon wounded at Walter Reed Army Medical Center and thanked blood donors at the Eisenhower Executive Office Building. She wrote two open letters—one to elementary school students and one to middle- and high-schoolers—offering them support and prodding them gently to be open about their feelings. The letters were sent to state superintendents across the country.

"I want to reassure you that there are many people—including your family, your teachers, and your school counselor—who are there to listen to you," she told the older students. To the younger ones, she suggested, "You can also write down your thoughts or draw a picture that shows how you are feeling and share that with the adults in your life." Laura went on five television networks and firmly told each news anchor that parents should turn off their television sets, to focus on sharing meals and reading bedtime stories. In thirty-six hours, she and presidential adviser Karen Hughes pulled together the moving memorial service at Washington National Cathedral for which Laura selected hymns that she felt would provide a balm for the soul. She squeezed her husband's hand when he rose to speak, and patted his leg when he sat back down. She traveled to western Pennsylvania and she bowed her head for those who had perished on Flight 93, then met for hours with the victims' families, staying until she had talked with every one.

While the president and his aides used the harsh rhetoric of war, the first lady offered quiet words of empathy and reassurance. "Of course I feel, like everyone does, sadness and anxiety," she said, calmly as always. "I also feel, I know, everything is being done to make sure America is safe. Because I know that, I feel reassured."

"She thinks about other people all the time," said Reverend Card. "She is constantly watching to see if other people are taken care of. That is a part of her. That is who she is." But while Laura had asked the pastor to be available to counsel her staff, the first lady did not take advantage of that opportunity herself.

I wondered who took care of her.

Without fanfare, Laura Bush became the first administration official to return to the nation's domestic agenda when she took her education summit on the road to Cincinnati a month after the attacks. The ambitious education reform effort seemed washed away in the aftermath of September 11 and the buildup to war against the Taliban. The first lady's effort assured those struggling to educate poor children that their own battlefield had not been forgotten. "I appreciate the first lady is out pushing this agenda," said a state administrator that day. "It speaks volumes to me that these priorities are not going to wait."

The newly visible first lady also began to speak out about the plight of Afghan women under the Taliban. Advocates around the world paid attention, hoping that they had found an activist for women's rights inside the conservative White House. In that, they were overly optimistic.

She was brave. "Freaked out, the girls are," the president told a rescue worker in New York that first week. "Wife's okay. She understands we're at war—got a war mentality, and so do I." While some Americans were frozen with fear over anthrax spores slipping through the mail slot and possible smallpox bombs, the first lady refused the vaccines offered to her. "I just didn't really feel like it was necessary," she told me, hastening to add, so as not to appear critical of anyone else, "I'm not suggesting that other people wouldn't want to. I didn't."

Her unrelieved public stoicism and her enormous capacity to feel took their toll. Flying back from her Cincinnati appearance, she seemed pensive and solemn, staring out the window of her jet, rubbing her temples. Her emotions were rubbed raw, she said, and left her sometimes fighting for control. She told me about a visit she and the president made to Pentagon burn victims at Washington Hospital Center, "and the commander-in-chief walked in, and one of the military men, his hands were totally wrapped and bandaged, and he tried to salute. I've had a lot of moments like that," she said.

"I met with teachers who actually had to run from their school. They were dealing with what we are all dealing with, but in such a very profound way, their personal fears and anxieties from the events as well as trying to think about it and somehow cope with the fears of the children," she reflected. She had picked a book to read to the children at that New York school, called "I Love You, Little One," and she knew it was, in ordinary times, below the level of a second-grader.

It was a story with a repeated refrain. "A bear, a cub, asked 'Do you love me, mama?' and the mama said 'I love you always and forever,' and a frog and a deer and a duck and finally, it ends with a child who asks. And the mother says 'I love you always and forever.' And I thought they might think it was slightly babyish. And they didn't. You could just tell. They wanted to hear that over and over again. Like all of us, really. Under these circumstances."

While the men who were the public face of the administration appeared daily to discuss bombing raids and anthrax deaths, Laura decided she would deal with emotional casualties. In a surprisingly stirring speech at the National Press Club, she said that "Americans are willing to fight and die for our freedoms, but more importantly, we are willing to live for them."

She talked a lot about how citizens' sense of self-absorption had faded, how strangers rushed to help each other out. She was buoyed by the money that children all over the country pressed into her hand, asking her to send it to the Afghan Children's Fund the White House had established. The Sunday after the attacks, the chaplain at Camp David had drawn his sermon from Psalm 27, and when she returned to the White House, Laura made it the verse to be printed on the official Christmas Card: "I believe I shall see the goodness of the Lord in the land of the living." It epitomized what she believed.

But her private responsibility, and the one she sees as her most important one, has been to remain an emotional bulwark for her husband.

She makes sure they have old friends come to visit at Camp David nearly every weekend, even when the president meets there with his war council. "The president and I have a lot of friends who we have had our whole life," she said. "They check in a lot. They call." His brother Marvin and his sister, Doro, and their spouses provided them with support. "That is very comforting for us," Laura said, "and I think this is really true for most families, to spend time with each other." More than once, when she needed to go out of town by herself, she would call one of the president's fraternity brothers. "Come stay with George," she would say. "Have dinner with him. Watch the game." The couple would try to eat dinner together most every night, then spend the evening doing, she said, what they always had done. In speech after speech, President Bush would credit his wife for her role soothing the nation, and indirectly, soothing him. She is a "rock," he liked to say. Laura would give herself no credit. "He acts like I steady him, but the truth is, he steadies me," she said. "We have a very sustaining relationship. It's always been that way. We like to be around each other."

They didn't skip meals. They got plenty of sleep. They were disciplined. That was how successful people, she figured, kept on an even keel. Upstairs in the family quarters, after days of relentless bad news—dismaying intelligence reports, bombings in Israel, saber rattling in North Korea, a shuttle crash—the commander-in-chief and the first lady played with the cat and dogs, Spot and Barney, the frisky Scottish terrier puppy he had given her for her birthday the year of the election. They didn't talk about the terrible business of the twenty-first-century war that consumed him and would mark his place in history. "That's what he talked about all day," said Laura. "That's what he's thinking about every minute he isn't home. But, and this may sound crazy, we have three pets we're crazy about. Since our children are not there with us to entertain us, we let our three pets entertain us."

On those frightening evenings when CNN blared attack news, he watched the ball game, while she read nearby and listened in. The sound of it had always soothed her, from childhood, the announcer calling out the balls and strikes during long, innocent summer days.

To ameliorate her own anxiety and maintain her calm, Laura started putting in miles walking on the treadmill. She hired a personal trainer. "I've been working out," she told those gathered at the Press Club. Then she turned to the side, and said with just a bit of coquetry, "Can y'all tell?"

She had a philosophy inspiring in its simplicity: Women needed to take care of themselves so they could take care of everybody else. Who takes care of her? There was my answer: She takes care of herself.

Laura Bush has her fears, it turned out. She does worry for her husband's life. The assassination of one president seared her memory when she was already devastated from killing her classmate. The attempted assassination of another one came while her father-in-law was vice president. Of course, she worried for her husband's life. There was no point in denying that. George would tell Laura every time the Secret Service reported a threat against him, and she would offer him calm reassurances. "But you can't help when you're married to the president, not to worry about his safety," she said.

When I asked her in the weeks after the attacks if she feared more terrorism, she said, "I don't really know how to answer that." She looked to Noelia Rodriguez, who reminded the first lady what she had said in the past about living in a different security climate. "We know our lives have changed," Laura said. "But we also know that terrorism is limited. And that is the point. It is more isolating and therefore more frightening. And destructive. When we do look at it rationally, then we know that the likelihood of any one of us to be unsafe is very, very small." But a year later, in an interview with Bob Woodward for his book *Bush at War,* Laura acknowledged just how frightened she had been that there would be another strike.

"I was up at night, I was worried," and then she pointed at the president and told Woodward, "He was too. I knew it." Bush's first impulse was to deny it, and then Laura gave her husband what Woodward described as "one of those looks that only a spouse can give—'c'mon, let's level'—and yes, he acknowledged, he was up at night."

The anecdote was a fascinating look into how fiercely protective Laura had become of her husband's image. She had waited a year to correct the record on something that bothered her terribly. About a month after the attacks, the Bushes sat for a lengthy interview with *Newsweek* to share some of their personal emotions from those days. Laura always was much leerier of these sorts of cathartic exercises than her husband. Her privacy was paramount to her, and she was the last to offer up their intimate moments for public consumption. The president was always more voluble about his feelings. Usually, he would do the talking during these sorts of exchanges, and she would sit and nod. In the interview, the president described how glad the couple had been to see each other after that long, chaotic day, after he returned from darting about the country on *Air Force One,* and she was released from her secret location. They had hugged, hard, and held each other, and when they eventually got into bed, the president fell right to sleep. It was a shocking admission that caused a great deal of chatter: He had gone right off to sleep? On one of the most tragic and traumatic days of American history? He didn't lie awake at night and agonize? With her unparalleled instinct for tone, Laura knew this might show her husband as unengaged, lacking in gravitas. And so she saw a chance with Woodward to redeem her husband. A year later, she wanted it known: George *had* lain awake, suffering. That was only right.

A ferocious consumer of several newspapers every day, Laura scoured them for references that bothered her and indications of how the administration's messages were received. One day, the *Post* ran a photograph of Bush giving a speech. He was standing in front of the presidential seal in such a way that only the tips of the sheaths were visible behind his head, and the inadvertent effect was that he appeared to be wearing horns. Laura had Karen Hughes call the paper to ask editors to be more careful; Laura thought the picture might be used to leaflet cafés all over the Arab world, anywhere someone wanted to portray the leader of the free world as a devil.

As a president now defined by crisis, George leaned on his wife more than ever. "You know, this is a moment of high drama, needless to say," he said. "And she couldn't have been more calm and resolved, almost placid, which was very reassuring to me. I can't imagine what it would be like had Laura been hysterical, highly emotional. . . . Never did she say, 'Get me out of here, what have you done this for, why are we here, it's a miserable experience. . . . It's your war, see you later.' "

And she toned down Bush's rhetoric, expanding her usual gentle admonishments on his mispronunciations and malapropisms. He sounded too much like a swaggering Wild West lawman when he declared that he wanted Osama bin Laden "dead or alive," and so she sidled up to him and said, "Bushie, are you gonna git 'im?" Asked why, she said primly, "I just didn't much care for it." He was blunter. "She didn't want to see me become too bellicose, react with bloodlust," he said. "I'll tell you this: She's not a shrinking violet. She doesn't get mad; she gets pointed. If I do something that needs to be toned down, she'll tell me." And more than once. That swagger would creep back into his unscripted remarks, and she had to call him on it again and again. And he listened. He trusts her completely.

The first lady's influence extended only to words, not the actions behind them. She has never presumed to advise him on substance as much as on style.

As ever, she refused to consider that she might be taking on a new role, a changed role, any sort of role at all. "She doesn't see it as a role," said press secretary Rodriguez. "She is responding to it as all other Americans do. If you can reach through the media, to help them be comforted and consoled at this time, then that is a tremendous responsibility that she wants to fulfill." Even later, after Laura had become the first presidential wife to deliver the weekly radio address, when I talked to Rodriguez about what I saw as Mrs. Bush's remarkable transformation, Rodriguez said, "Don't use that word. She hates that word, 'transformation.' "

For Laura, it was important to believe that the way she behaved was the way she had always behaved, even as she admitted she was surprised when a friend said she was envious of her. "Why envious?" Laura asked. "Because you have a chance to actually do something," her friend replied, and Laura admitted that, yes, perhaps, at her midlife, with her children gone and with the nation facing enormous challenges, she could embrace a new direction for herself.

At the year's anniversary of the attacks, we talked about how her life had changed. Her husband was hammering the message month after month: The war against terror would last for a long time. We would not shrink from the war. We were at war, make no mistake about it.

"Do you see yourself as a wartime first lady?" I asked her.

Eleanor Roosevelt had rallied the nation to civil defense in World War II. Edith Wilson had grown sheep on the White House lawn and sold their wool to benefit the Red Cross in World War I. Not that I was suggesting Laura should do the same.

"No," she said immediately. "This is the first time that anyone has asked me that. We are at war, of course. I guess I just have never thought of it just exactly like you just asked it," she said. "You know I don't really think of myself as first lady, right?"

It was as if the position should not be exploited to its widest advantage. It was as if personal growth was suspect, as if seizing opportunity were opportunistic, as if transformation meant one was no longer faithful to one's roots, and one's self.

CHAPTER NINE

❧

War and Poetry

> *There's nothing political about American literature.*
>
> —Laura Bush

As the wife of the governor of Texas, Laura had learned she could live with integrity quite apart from her husband's ideology. She could successfully pursue a life of the mind independent of his political philosophies. She would invite writers to participate in her festival and other events, and, once they got over their shock, they would get to know her personally. They would come to recognize that her love for books was genuine. They would develop respect for how deeply she read. They would grow fond of her warmth and sincerity; they would be won over by that realness of hers. All of that could transcend deep divides they might have with her husband over the death penalty, gun control, women's reproductive rights. Laura's own positions were deliberately vague—*"If I differ from my husband, I'm not going to tell you"*—and folks always were too polite to ask. It didn't seem right. By the time she moved in at 1600 Pennsylvania Avenue, Laura could count among her friends many writers and authors who had grave reservations about her husband's presidency. But the strength of her personal relationships transcended all that.

Why couldn't that work for her in Washington? In the beginning, she seemed able to follow the identical pattern, and people were inclined to be receptive to her and respectful of her position. If the White House called or sent out engraved invitations on cream vellum, folks responded. Laura hit upon the idea of establishing her own sort of literary salon, an assembly of scholars and thinkers on a particular period of literature. It would be like a graduate seminar in comparative literature, but of the very highest order, under the grand moldings and gold leaf of the East Room. It would be carried on the cable channel C-SPAN, so that bibliophiles all across America could watch. It would confer an imprimatur of utmost importance to the topic, since it was being held in the White House, and, at the same time, it would sustain and nourish her intellect. The ceremonial life was a constricted one, she was learning, governed by protocol and rigid scheduling. There were only so many times one could admire handcrafted Christmas ornaments sent in from some craft cooperative. If she wanted meaningful dialogue, intellectual stimulation, and social discourse, she had to create it for herself.

Laura chose three areas to explore, and she picked her authors and historians and biographers carefully. Just as in Austin, those who received invitations were flabbergasted. But they swallowed, and, out of deference, they attended. Again, they came, they saw, and she conquered them. She started with Mark Twain, in November of 2001, because, she said, "I believe that Mark Twain is the first real American writer. . . . I think Mark Twain really talks about everything that is at the crux of what America is, even now." Next, in March 2002, she held a symposium that focused on the Harlem Renaissance, stood right there under the opulent chandeliers and quoted Zora Neale Hurston: "I have been in sorrow's kitchen and licked out all the pots." Hearing this apparently dutiful Republican woman reciting those words flew in the face of all the expectations of those gathered there. She loved the biting, soaring, strident Langston Hughes, and she read from his poetry in her opening remarks, too. She introduced David Levering Lewis, who won two

Pulitzer Prizes for his work on W. E. B. Du Bois, and then she settled back into her chair in the front row where she always sat for
these affairs, her eyes lit up with excitement. Hughes biographer
Arnold Rampersad was there, and he overheard her talking about
what writers she wanted for the next symposium, on women writers
of the West. "She talked about Willa Cather and Katherine Anne
Porter," Rampersad said. "That was when it became very clear that
she was seeing this world from the inside, not the outside." He
knew he was listening to a real reader.

The Western women came next, in September of 2002. In many
ways, they were Laura Welch Bush's first literary love. Those
women were her stock; they wrote of the struggles against the land
and the transcendent power of faith and love. "Laura Ingalls Wilder
delighted generations of readers with accounts of her family's
rugged and nomadic life in the West," she said, in her introductory
remarks. "My mother and I spent countless hours reading the Little
House series together." And here again she shocked those who had
formed notions about her based strictly on what they might have
gleaned from *Good Housekeeping*.

The girl from harsh, close-knit, segregated Midland, the woman
who always revered her roots, also betrayed her knowledge of more
troubling Texas themes. She adored Edna Ferber, for instance, a Hungarian Jewish shopkeeper's daughter from Milwaukee, who started out
writing for a newspaper in the early 1900s. "In my home state of
Texas," said Laura, "she is known for her sizzling novel *Giant,* which
was published in 1952. The characters may have been the product of
her first visit to the state, when she was reportedly shocked by the food,
the heat, and the swaggering arrogance of men in ten-gallon hats."

Ferber was even more scathing than that. Her *Giant* was "quite
a penetrating, mocking portrait of Texas rich people, and particularly of people making their money in oil," said Patricia Nelson
Limerick, the author of a revisionist history of Western conquest,
who was invited to speak. "I did Mrs. Bush a terrible disservice

thinking that maybe she didn't know," she said, after the first lady's remarks on Ferber, "that she thought these were all little houses on the prairie."

An additional convocation on libraries featured Vartan Gregorian, the former president of the New York Public Library and Brown University, who gave an impassioned account of the history of the communal reading room and its origins in Alexandria. This time Laura, in a pink linen suit, sat beside her mother-in-law, in her trademark pearls, and again listened keenly. She quoted from William H. Gass's essay "In Defense of the Book":

"The library is meant to satisfy the curiosity of the curious, provide a place for the lonely where they may enjoy companionship and warmth of the word. The library supplies handbooks for the handy, novels for insomniacs, scholarship for the scholarly, and makes available works of literature to those people they will eventually haunt so successfully."

To Laura, reading is not primarily a communal pursuit. It can be; she might read aloud a paragraph from the morning papers to her husband after he brings them to her with coffee each daybreak in bed. That is how they have started their days for years. They end their days with books in bed as well. Reading for pleasure, she once said, is her one vice. "Laura, for God's sake, turn off the light!" she says the president often tells her. She is an avid reader for information and gives herself assigned reading, to learn about her husband's poll ratings or to brief herself on political personalities or the intricacies of policies. Sometimes, she reveals a glimpse of just how deeply she reads and retains. Before hosting an event for governors' spouses in January of 2003, she flipped through a briefing book. Each state got a page, which contained a photo of the spouse and a short biography. When Laura got to Hawaii, she caught the mistake: The photo was of a woman, when it should have been a man. "This is wrong," she said. "Hawaii elected a woman." Which matters to her. She would never overtly say so. But there it is.

For Laura, reading for pleasure is a solitary pursuit, a refuge, a diversion, an intimate act carried out in private. Her husband has a direct and personal relationship with Jesus Christ. Laura has a direct and personal relationship with the written word, whether it be drugstore thriller or challenging literary fiction. "I imagine every person who loves to read can think back on points of their life, with great nostalgia, when you remember the summer, for instance, that you read all the Russian writers," she said. At their Crawford ranch, floor-to-ceiling bookshelves flank the breezeway. His are filled with baseball books. Hers are filled with the classics and her collection of children's literature.

Reading was comforting, and "something to do when you were an only child." Literature is "hauntingly quiet," she said. "Writers write and readers read in solitude."

But the world intruded on her, as it inevitably did, ever since she had made the choice to give up her own career to join her husband in his congressional bid. "Everyone can like American literature, no matter what your party." But literature was not apolitical, and she probably really had known that all along. She just tried to keep it as her little secret, in a White House that seemed increasingly driven by ideology.

When the bombs first fell on Afghanistan that Sunday in October of 2001, the nation was tense but remarkably unified. The case for war was clear to the American people. Al Qaeda had executed an act of unimaginable monstrosity; its leader, Osama bin Laden, was being harbored by the Taliban, the controlling authority of Afghanistan; that government had to be eliminated. In an effort to persuade the hearts and minds of Arabs in the Middle East, Laura joined the administration's effort to speak out for the rights of Afghan women. There was no basis in the Koran for the Taliban's subjugation of women, and Laura said as much when she delivered the president's weekly radio address that November. Typically, she voiced surprise that no other first lady had done so before.

It was a bold new deployment of Laura, masterminded by the female communications strategists of the war effort—adviser Karen Hughes, vice presidential aide Mary Matalin, Pentagon spokeswoman Torie Clark, and Charlotte Beers, a former Madison Avenue executive who had been hired at the State Department to influence opinion in the Arab world. When I asked Laura about that, she refused to give any indication of message manipulation behind the scenes.

"How did you decide to take on Afghan women's rights?" I asked.

"Well, I mean, I don't . . . well, it just seemed the right thing to do," she said.

Reading into the radio microphone, in her low, soft Texas voice, Laura said: "Women have been denied access to doctors when they're sick. Life under the Taliban is so hard and repressive, even small displays of joy are outlawed—children aren't allowed to fly kites; their mothers face beatings for laughing out loud. Women cannot work outside the home, or even leave their homes by themselves."

Who could argue with that? No respect for cultural diversity could be extended to a regime so repressive. It was Laura's first foray as outspoken advocate, called into service by her husband's handlers, and it left some women's activists hungering for more.

She took up the theme again and again, through that winter after the attacks. Laura Bush actually gave Americans an assignment in the war against terror: She asked them to contribute money to an Afghan children's fund, and to send school supplies so that children could go back to school. The first lady took her message on the road, on her first solo trip abroad, to Paris, Budapest, and Prague, where she delivered the first Radio Free Europe address to Afghanistan. Laura moved beyond the role she had occupied as comforter-in-chief and became outspoken. Her travels alone, nine months after the attacks, coincided with horrifying episodes of inhumanity, and she seemed suffused with, if not exactly candor, a new freedom to exhibit the clarity of emotion and thought that she displayed in her private life.

On the flight to Europe, she read that seventeen children were among the victims of a Chechnya bombing, and she decided to revise her speech on the spot. Karen Hughes, who already had announced she was resigning as the president's aide and returning to Austin, was on the trip with Laura, and she helped her rewrite it. The first lady wanted to decry a culture of rage that incubated young suicide bombers, a topic way outside her usual domain. Speaking to the Organisation for Economic Co-operation and Development in Paris, she said, "Every teacher, every parent, every leader has a responsibility to condemn the terrible tragedy of children blowing themselves up to kill others. Education can help children see beyond a world of hate and hopelessness."

In an interview after the speech, Laura said she had been moved by the horror of children struck down while parading for freedom in Russia, and from there she waded into the Mideast debate without trepidation. "It's so easy to empathize with families in Israel and around the world who would literally be afraid to send their children to the grocery story or the bowling alley" for fear of suicide bombers, she said. Asked about the Palestinians, she was ready with an answer before the question was even posed: "Can I empathize with a mother who sends her child out to kill herself and others? No." Then she paused and employed a diplomat's moderation: "You have to have sympathy for both sides, and all of us in the world need to urge both of them—the Palestinians and Israelis—to try to stop the violence and come to the table."

Her travels through Europe over those ten days seemed a study in the gore and glory of human history, and she immersed herself in them. She seemed to be making field observations in the age-old paradoxes still shaping the global conflict that had plunged her husband's presidency into crisis. In Paris, she visited the Louvre and the Musée D'Orsay, with its renowned collection of Impressionists, suffused with light. But she also lingered over a collection of Afghan art that had been saved and displayed at the Guimet. She regarded the drawings of massive Buddhas similar to those blown to bits by the Taliban. In Budapest, she toured an exhibit devoted to one thousand years of Christianity. In the Czech Republic, she added to her schedule a visit to Theresienstadt, the Nazi concentration camp outside Prague where 140,000 Jews were processed for deportation to death camps. In Prague itself, she dined in one of the city's trendiest new restaurants, before stepping across the street and into the ghostly old Jewish ghetto, spared during World War II only because Hitler was determined to create an "exotic museum of an extinct race." As she threaded her way through the narrow cobblestone streets, delighted Japanese tourists thronged after her, their cameras clicking away. She was particularly keen to meet with Czech Republic president Václav Havel. "He was a playwright, he was an intellectual. He was not someone you would think of becoming the president," she said. "His life story symbolizes the opening of Central Europe after the fall of communism."

As it happened, while she was away, the husband who depended on her steadiness found himself swept up in one of the periodic political squalls. News reports questioned whether he had been informed of the intelligence warning of attacks by hijacked aircraft weeks before September 11. Half a world away, Laura leapt to his defense. "I think it is very sad that people would play upon the victims' emotions" by suggesting her husband missed some clues prior to the tragedy, she said in Budapest, and she leaned forward, her body coiled, her speech empathetic. The briefing in question was "so inspecific that there was no way that you could have predicted what would happen. . . . I know my husband. And all Americans know how he has acted in Afghanistan and in the war with terror. I think really, we need to put this in perspective." Her message was quite clear: I trust him, and so should you.

But even as she seemed to become more forthright about what she might really believe, in her own, independent soul, Laura became more deft at avoiding what she did not want to say as a public figure, if it might conflict in even the smallest way with official U.S. positions.

Asked about her view of women's rights in Saudi Arabia, a U.S. ally where women are forbidden to drive and own property, and where religious police were known to swat women who appeared on the streets not fully covered, she pointed out that girls "do attend school there." Later, on the first anniversary of the attacks, I asked her if she might be taking her exhortations to other countries where women struggled for full participation in society. She sat silent.

"Like Saudi Arabia," I said.

"I know where you are going with your question," she said, and she laughed, "and you are asking the wrong person."

Asked about religious schools—madrasas—that teach Islamic fundamentalism in Pakistan and Saudi Arabia, home countries of fifteen of the nineteen alleged September 11 hijackers, Mrs. Bush was careful not to criticize those two allies crucial to her husband's anti-terror coalition.

"I think we can work with all of the countries that have madrasas and encourage them to make sure that the madrasas also include a mainstream education. A lot of the madrases do, anyway. It's, I think, a smaller percentage that are so one-sided or so limited in their scope of education," she said.

When she and the president invited Saudi Crown Prince Abdullah to their Texas ranch, she did not take the opportunity to raise such issues with the Saudi leader, she said. And she did not attend the leaders' meetings.

But, in a private White House meeting with a group of Saudi women some months ago, she said she did discuss women's rights and the cultural differences between the United States and Saudi Arabia. "I respect the differences that we have in our cultures and what they believe," she said.

She would approach, and then retreat. At a cancer hospital in Budapest, where the first lady learned that Hungarian women with breast cancer often were so stigmatized that they would not ask for help, she called for women across the world to get "access to important health information and resources." But pressed to square that with the administration's refusal to release a scheduled $34 million in U.S. contributions to the United Nations Population Fund, she hedged her answer. The president had said the organization, which offers family planning, HIV prevention, and maternal health programs, might be involved in forced abortions in China, an allegation repeatedly leveled by Christian fundamentalists and repeatedly rebutted as baseless by U.N. officials. As soon as the question was out of Associated Press reporter Sandra Sobieraj's mouth, Laura immediately said, "I don't think it's the entire $34 million," suggesting she had been monitoring an issue of some concern to her. Then she caught herself. "I understand the administration's position on it," she said, an interesting finesse, since she avoided saying whether she agreed or disagreed with that position. Pushed to say if she believed the U.N. group is involved in abortion, she professed: "I really don't know that much about that issue."

In another discussion with those of us traveling with her through Europe, she laughed off an invitation to contradict the president's opposition to putting U.S. peacekeepers in Afghanistan. She had just finished a meeting where aid workers in that country had implored her for just that.

"I think I'll defer to the president, and to the secretary of state, and to the secretary of defense, and to the national security adviser, and all of those other people, first, before I make any recommendations," Mrs. Bush said.

Hungary's *Népszabadság* newspaper asked about the political advice she gives the president.

"Obviously, I'm not his adviser. I'm his wife," she said.

This approach and retreat was not confined to issues offshore. As librarians across the nation began to assess the ramifications of the hastily passed Patriot Act, they spoke out against provisions that seemed to permit the government to look at library patrons' book-borrowing histories and Internet usage. The 64,000-member American Library Association passed a resolution in opposition to "any use of governmental power to suppress . . . or to intimidate individuals exercising free inquiry." The former librarian in the White House remained silent.

As the Bush administration moved through its first term, and the economy foundered, and states plunged into record deficits, the Bushes' signature issue of education reform fell to pieces. A scandal of book cooking in Houston, where Education Secretary Rod Paige had served as superintendent, threw into question the White House's push on standardized testing for assessment. Bush had argued that such rigorous measures had driven up performance among Houston students. An audit revealed that those improvements were phony, since hundreds of students who had failed the tests had then dropped out. Laura Bush's ally Senator Edward Kennedy, who had praised her efforts and pushed the "No Child Left Behind" Education Reform Bill through the Senate, now bitterly inveighed against the law. The president had failed to provide the funding necessary to meet the government's sweeping mandate, he said. The reform was a sham. The National Education Association, representing 2.7 million of the country's teachers, announced plans to sue the federal government, arguing that schools should not be forced to pay for the law's extensive requirements. "A power struggle is going on," NEA president Reg Weaver told his membership. "The feds are squeezing the states, states are squeezing the school districts, and they're trying to squeeze you. What we're saying is, it's time to squeeze back."

And Laura? She would take no part in any power struggle. Instead, she called on local communities to pick up the slack, urging business to sponsor programs and parents to help out. "Parents need to be involved and support teachers, whether it's providing a quiet space where their children can learn or baking cupcakes for Valentine's Day," she said. On the topic she held most dear, education, the first lady with the graduate degree seemed to have made a full retreat to an earlier era. She was certainly in a better position than her husband to think through such issues as the teaching of reading and the impact on students and schools of high-stakes testing. She was in a position, actually, to bring the president some news. What if she had given deep thought to the statistics coming out of the Houston school district, the basis of so much of the so-called Texas miracle of achievement? Laura Bush certainly has that kind of mind. That is within the realm of what she could do. It is even within the realm of what, as a woman who cares deeply about education, she might have been expected to do. She could have stayed involved, and delved more thoroughly into the details. She could have questioned.

But in the end, she is an old-fashioned first lady. She moves in the directions she is asked to move. Goes where she is told. Nobody urges her to do otherwise. Nobody stopped her when she used her platform to urge cupcake baking.

As the Pentagon readied the nation's massive military for an invasion of Iraq, Laura planned for poetry. She wanted to feature the work of favorite poets Langston Hughes, Walt Whitman, and Emily Dickinson at her fourth literary symposium. Unlike the U.S. overthrow of the Taliban, the pending war on Iraq opened up a chasm in American public opinion. It is unfathomable that Laura Bush, careful reader, failed to recognize the collision course that war and poetry were on. She naively believed she could move safely out of the way. Instead, the first casualty of the war was her literary showcases.

The first lady had called upon poetry to comfort her during the fighting in Afghanistan, she said in her speech at the National Press Club. She noted she had read from the works of the nation's poet laureate, Billy Collins. And so the invitations went out to poets across the nation for the symposium, scheduled for February 12, 2003. One of those who received the invite, Sam Hamill, saw an opportunity for an antiwar protest. Hamill, the founder of the small Copper Canyon Press in Port Townsend, Washington, had no personal relationship with the first lady, and no way to distinguish her efforts from those of her husband, who Hamill thought was leading the country into an immoral war. He wasn't honored to receive an invitation from the White House. Instead, he said, he was "overcome by a wave of nausea." He sent an e-mail message to fifty colleagues asking them to send him antiwar poems and protests, which would be compiled into an anthology and presented to the first lady at the event. His efforts struck a nerve in the overwhelmingly left-of-center literary community, and the poems began pouring in. Within days, Hamill was swamped with thousands of submissions, including offerings from some of America's better-known poets.

As the effort gathered steam, the White House learned of Hamill's intentions from another poet invited to the event. Laura abruptly canceled the symposium. Her office issued a statement: "While Mrs. Bush respects and believes in the right of all Americans to express their opinions, she, too, has opinions, and believes that it would be inappropriate to turn what is intended to be a literary event into a political forum."

Poets promptly announced plans to read the antiwar messages anyway, and they joined their voices to an increasingly loud chorus of protesters. Much of their anger was directed at Laura Bush. In Manchester, Vermont, Jamaica Kincaid thanked the first lady "for being so thin-skinned, or we would not be sitting here today." Julia Alvarez, who had been invited to the event, said she sat right down after its cancellation on January 30 and wrote a poem titled "The

White House Has Disinvited Poets." The Pulitzer Prize winner Galway Kinnell noted what he called "a little perception and warning" from Emily Dickinson: "Assent, and you are sane. Demur, you are straightaway dangerous and handled with a chain saw." Even Billy Collins, who had stood side by side with the first lady in support of her literacy programs, spoke out against the war.

Hamill scoffed at the first lady for failing to recognize that the works of Hughes, Whitman, and Dickinson could not be examined without limning the poets' own political views. And he was wrong about that, of course. Laura Bush knew full well how disappointed the three could be in their country; she had read their works. She understood them. As Collins explained, "I think the loss in this particular case was the opportunity to look at Whitman and Dickinson. In the middle of both of their lives occurred the central trauma of our country, the Civil War. And Whitman more or less jumped into action. He served as a volunteer nurse and wrote a poem, 'Vigil Strange I Kept on the Field One Night,' where he holds the body of a dead boy and buries him. Whereas Emily Dickinson just stuck to her knitting, and her knitting just happened to do with immortality and death and the grave. It is a wonderful demonstration of the choice that poets have, to deal with the world around them in whatever way they think best."

"Poetry and the American Voice" would have ventured into that territory, in all likelihood, had it not been derailed by folks announcing they would show up and be outright rude.

The final irony of the cancellation was that the first lady got far more attention for something she didn't do than for anything she ever did.

Laura Bush is more like Emily Dickinson in dealing with the world the way she thinks best. As a first lady in wartime, she has resisted the pleas from some quarters that she whisper wisdoms to the president on staying the course in Afghanistan, or returning funding to libraries and education, or bolstering rights for women right here in America. She is not an activist by temperament. And she bristles when she is portrayed, especially by her husband, as a model of old-fashioned wifedom. When he apologized to a campaign crowd in 2002 for Laura's absence on the congressional election trail, he said she had to stay in Crawford and "sweep the porch." Asked later, on that very porch, with him by her side, whether she appreciated the remark, she shook her head and mouthed "No." Yet, above all else, she is a loyal wife whose first priority is to support her husband in risky times.

This trait dismays and disappoints some observers, but a strong expression of support comes from her predecessor, Hillary Rodham Clinton.

"It's been more the tradition than the exception that first ladies have figured out other ways to be helpful than to have direct impact on policy," said Clinton. "In several key instances she has tried to carve that out, with respect to the women of Afghanistan and emphasizing teacher training. I think that gave her a lot of satisfaction and impact.

"But the real priority has to be to support your husband in the pressing business of being president. You just have to be there to further the agenda that is the top priority of the White House, and certainly under these circumstances," and she was talking about the din of war, "nothing else much is being heard anyway."

It is a very complicated calculation, the business of being first lady. It requires a woman to figure out a way to be true to herself and to make a contribution, and that, really, is an accommodation that all women make their whole lives long, adapting and adjusting, composing a life for themselves amid the relationships with those they love and sustain.

What guides Laura Bush are the choices she made years ago, when she joined her path with George W. Bush. Supporting that man she loves, she once told me, "is the most important part of my job, whether my husband is president or not."

ACKNOWLEDGMENTS

This book could not have been completed without the steadfast support of many people.

I am fortunate to have smart and generous colleagues at *The Washington Post,* a newspaper that, as an institution, embraces book writing. I am especially grateful to Gene Robinson, Deborah Heard, and Steve Reiss of the Style section, and certainly to David Von Drehle; they all gave me an opportunity to grow on their pages, and then they let me go off and chance another form. My thanks to Len Downie and Tom Wilkinson, and to Steve Coll, who patiently explained his own system for book organization. Robin Groom is, simply, invaluable. I owe a particular debt to the esteemed Henry Allen, who always launches me into some higher altitude of thought and encourages me to rely on my ear.

My agent, Rafe Sagalyn, has guided this project from the start with humor and confidence and excellent advice. At Simon and Schuster, David Rosenthal has urged me into print with his particular profane good cheer, and Ruth Fecych has been a dream as an editor, fine with words and insights, thoughtful, calm, and meticulous. I've benefited from the energy of Aileen Boyle and Marie Florio.

Many friends have given me their best wishes and encouragement and endured my distance. Dale Russakoff, Karen Heller, Kevin Merida, and Annie Groer have ruminated on my subject with me. Michael Powell has let me yammer at him incessantly, through cyberspace, about everything else in the world. Sally Jenkins is the steadfast friend who cajoled me on all those occasions when I wanted to throw the laptop through the window; she and Nicole Bengiveno offered me a much-needed writing retreat.

I owe most of what I am to my parents. From my father I inherited an ear for the music and syncopation of words. From my mother I learned empathy and critical regard for a person's underlying motivations, including, most importantly, my own.

Finishing a book is lovely, but Sara, Sofia, and Bill are my life's work, and my joy. Michael Sokolove is the perfect husband, honest to God.

SOURCES

The vast majority of the information in this biography has been informed by my own reporting on, observation of, and experiences with Laura Bush over the course of two and a half years. As the *Washington Post* reporter assigned to cover Mrs. Bush, I have traveled with her domestically and internationally and interviewed her extensively since inauguration day 2001. I've attended numerous White House events she hosted and organized. Under my byline, nineteen articles about her have appeared in the *Washington Post*.

In early 2002, I met with Noelia Rodriguez, Mrs. Bush's press secretary, to outline my hopes and goals for the project and to ask for cooperation from the first lady. I was determined to treat Mrs. Bush with seriousness and to focus on what had shaped her; her grace in building a life for herself intrigued me. I wanted to interview her specifically for the book, and I asked that she might direct me to the people she felt knew her best and had observed her during different periods of her life. Through Rodriguez, Mrs. Bush asked that I write her a letter further detailing the book and reiterating my requests. I did so. She never responded, which I find surprising, since she is meticulous in answering all sorts of correspondence. The word was passed back to me that Karen Hughes, then a special adviser to the president and his specialist in message control, had decreed that Mrs. Bush would not sit for interviews specific to this book. I have never received an explanation for this decision, and Hughes failed to return several phone calls I made to her office. The White House had no quarrel with my newspaper coverage of the first lady; I continued to enjoy excellent access to Mrs. Bush and her staff, and I continued to interview her and travel with her.

This position has not been a hindrance, however. I have interviewed more than a hundred people about Laura Bush. Some of those, including Bush family members, administration officials, and a few friends, have spoken with me frankly only on condition that their remarks not be attributed. I also have relied on public records and previously published books and newspaper and magazine articles, as well as broadcast interview transcripts. Where I have utilized another writer's insights or conclusions or language, I have tried to take care to credit him or her with the text. Where anecdotes and quotations have been widely recounted, I have tried to cite the original source below.

The biography *First Son* by Bill Minutaglio has given me invaluable insight into the development and character of George W. Bush; *Ambling into History,* by Frank Bruni, provided great detail on the role of Laura Bush in the winning presidential campaign.

I relied on *Laura: America's First Lady, First Mother* by Antonia Felix, for the recollections of Jenna Welch and family history; on *Whatever the Wind Delivers* by Janet M. Neugebauer and Walt McDonald, for its vivid portrayal of Texas social history; and on *Hidden Power: Presidential Marriages That Shaped Our Recent History* by Kati Marton, for guiding my thinking on the impact of a first lady on her husband and her country. Many times while creating this portrait I turned to my dog-eared copy of *Composing a Life* by Mary Catherine Bateson, and read again her passionate arguments for allowing the possibility that achievement and creativity flow in fits and starts, especially for women, as they adapt themselves to those around them. *Texas Monthly* editor Paul Burka was generous with his reflections and insights into the Bush marriage during the couple's years in the Austin Governor's Mansion. I was made to feel very welcome in Midland and in Austin, where folks went out of their way to, as they would say, visit with me on the subject of Laura Bush. I would like to especially thank Steve and Peggy Buck, Bobby and Denise

Burns, Dr. Viola Coleman, Earle and Dottie Craig, Lynn and Bill Munn, and Babe and Marilyn Schwartz.

Published sources follow:

Bilyeau, Nancy, "Meet the Next First Lady," *Good Housekeeping,* October 2000.

Bonnin, Julie, "What Laura Wants," *Austin American-Statesman,* April 19, 1999.

J. Bottum, "The Poets vs. The First Lady," *Weekly Standard,* February 17, 2003.

Brant, Martha, "Comforter in Chief," *Newsweek,* December 3, 2001.

Brisson, Lynn, "First-Grade Students Are Flat Out Proud to Hear from First Lady," *Greensboro News & Record,* April 6, 2003.

Brooks, A. Phillip, "Education Bill's Passage Is Laura Bush's First Big Move," *Austin American-Statesman,* June 22, 1999.

Bruni, Frank, "Quiet Strength: For Laura Bush, a Direction She Never Wished to Go In," *New York Times,* July 31, 2000.

Bumiller, Elisabeth, "As World Waits, Quiet on the West Wing Front," *New York Times,* March 17, 2003.

———, "Quietly, the First Lady Builds a Literary Room of Her Own," *New York Times,* October 7, 2002.

———, "With Antiwar Poetry Set, Mrs. Bush Postpones Event," *New York Times,* January 31, 2003.

Burka, Paul, "The Education of Laura Bush," *Texas Monthly,* April 2001.

———, "The W. Nobody Knows," *Texas Monthly,* June 1999.

Bush, George W., remarks during walking tour of the ranch with press pool, White House official transcript, January 2, 2003.

Bush, Laura, transcript of National Press Club Luncheon speech, November 8, 2001.

Couric, Katie, Interview of Laura Bush, *Today,* NBC, January 19, 2001.

Court, Ayesha, "Book Festival Soldiers on in Edgy D.C.," *USA Today,* October 14, 2002.

Curtis, Gregory, "At Home with Laura," *Time,* January 8, 2001.

Davidson, John, "Just a Surprising Person," *San Antonio Express-News,* January 19, 2001.

Douglas, Jack, Jr., "Bush Friend Taken from Tarrant Jail," *Fort Worth Star-Telegram,* March 1, 2001.

Emery, Noemie, "First Dad: The Burden of Having a President as Father," *Weekly Standard,* June 16, 2003.

Feldman, Claudia, "First Lady," *Houston Chronicle,* July 20, 1997.

Friedman, Barbara, "In Wartime, Being 'Just Laura' Isn't Enough," *Baltimore Sun,* March 19, 2003.

Friedman, Kinky, "The Houseguest," *Texas Monthly,* October 2002.

Gamerman, Ellen, "A Novel Take on Political Life," *Baltimore Sun,* January 16, 2001.

Gangel, Jamie, Interview of Laura Bush, *Today,* NBC, September 27, 1999.

"George W. Bush: Portrait of a Candidate," *CNN Newsstand,* August 4, 2000.

Goad, Kimberly, "Laura Bush: Adjusting to Spotlight, the First Lady Relishes Her Role," *Dallas Morning News,* September 24, 1995.

Good, Regan, "Questions for Billy Collins," *New York Times,* February 23, 2003.

Heath, Jena, "First Lady Laura Bush," *Atlanta Journal-Constitution,* June 10, 2001.

Hollandsworth, Skip, "Reading Laura Bush," *Texas Monthly,* November 1996.

Hornaday, Ann, and Michele Stanush, "Celebrating Texas Authors," *Austin American-Statesman,* November 17, 1996.

Howd, Aimee, "Top Candidates' Top Valentines," *Insight on the News,* February 14, 2000.

Jennings, Diane, "Finding Spirituality on the Farm," *Dallas Morning News,* April 28, 2002.

Johnson, Darragh, and Justin Blum, "Living a Librarian's Dream," *Washington Post,* January 20, 2001.

Keen, Judy, "Laura Bush: Calm Amid the Chaos," *USA Today,* July 31, 2001.

Kelly, Lee, "Laura Bush, First Lady of Texas," *Austin American-Statesman,* September 24, 1995.

King, Larry, Interview of Laura Bush, *Larry King Live,* CNN, April 18, 2001.

————, Interview of Bob Woodward, *Larry King Live,* CNN, November 18, 2002.

Kipen, David, "A Literary Alamo," *San Francisco Chronicle,* January 17, 2001.

Kristof, Nicholas D., "George W. Bush's Journey: A Boy from Midland," *New York Times,* May 21, 2000.

————, "Learning How to Run: A West Texas Stumble," *New York Times,* July 27, 2000.

"Lee High School Senior Dies in Traffic Mishap," *Midland Reporter-Telegram,* November 7, 1963.

Leonard, Mary, "Behind Scenes, Mrs. Bush Has a Pivotal Role," *Boston Globe,* July 31, 2000.

Long, Colleen, "Bush: Parents Should Pick Up Slack After Budget Cuts," Associated Press, May 22, 2003.

Loven, Jennifer, "President a Proud Husband, but Public Displays of Admiration for First Lady Not Always on the Mark," Associated Press, October 28, 2002.

McLeese, Don, "Book Event Was Too Noble for Cynicism," *Austin American-Statesman,* November 19, 1996.

McQuillan, Laurence, and Judy Keen, "Texas White House," *USA Today,* April 13, 2001.

Mehren, Elizabeth, "Verse by Verse, a Plea for Peace," *Los Angeles Times,* February 17, 2003.

"Miss Welch, Bush Wed in Methodist Rites," *Midland Reporter-Telegram,* November 6, 1977.

Noonan, Peggy, "Be Proud of What We Stand For," *Ladies' Home Journal,* October 2003.

Orlean, Susan, "A Place Called Midland," *The New Yorker,* October 16, 2000.

Pollitt, Katha, "Poetry Makes Nothing Happen?" *The Nation,* February 24, 2003.

Pooley, Eric, "How George Got His Groove," *Time,* June 21, 1999.

Press, Joy, "Bards Not Bombs in NYC," *The Village Voice,* February 25, 2003.

Racine, Marty, "His Hometown," *Houston Chronicle,* February 25, 2001.

Ragavan, Chitra, "Safety First," *U.S. News & World Report,* September 9, 2002.

Reed, Julia, "First in Command," *Vogue,* June 2001.

————, "The Son Also Rises," *Weekly Standard,* February 10, 1997.

Romano, Lois, "Laura Bush: A Twist on Traditional," *Washington Post,* May 14, 2000.

————, "A Run for the House," *Washington Post,* July 29, 1999.

Romano, Lois, and George Lardner, Jr., "1986: A Life-Changing Year," *Washington Post,* July 25, 1999.

Rush, George, and Joanna Molloy, "Hudson Hawk Takes on the Doves," *New York Daily News,* February 27, 2003.

Russert, Tim, "Governor George Bush and His Wife, Laura Bush, Talk About Their Past, the Present, and Their Hopes for the Future," CNBC, December 30, 2000.

Schiller, Laura, and Melanie Verveer, "War Puts Demands on First Ladies, Too," *Los Angeles Times,* April 6, 2003.

Schindehette, Susan, "The First Lady Next Door," *People,* January 29, 2001.

————, "What a Difference a Year Makes," *People,* January 21, 2002.

Schwartz, Maryln, "Next Stop Austin," *Dallas Morning News,* January 16, 1995.

Sciolino, Elaine, "Transition in Washington: The New First Lady," *New York Times,* January 20, 2001.

Shipman, Claire, Interview of Laura Bush, *Good Morning America,* ABC, May 1, 2002.

Smith, Dinitia, "Laureates Convene, Waxing Poetic," *New York Times,* April 28, 2003.

Smith, Lynn, "A Place Called Midland," *Los Angeles Times,* September 7, 2000.

————, "At Home on the Trail," *Los Angeles Times,* July 31, 2000.

Stamberg, Susan, "Laura Bush on the Importance of Reading," *Morning Edition,* National Public Radio, July 31, 2001.

"Sour Notes Over Mottola Bucks," *New York Post,* July 29, 2003.

Tapper, Jake, "The Last Place We Liberated," *Salon,* April 10, 2003.

Temple, Georgia, *Midland Reporter-Telegram,* February 14, 2002.

————, *Midland Reporter-Telegram,* September 5, 2002.

Toppo, Greg, "Teachers' Union Plans to Sue Federal Government Over States' Funding of Education Law," *USA Today,* July 3, 2003.

Unsigned editorial, "Leave Education to Iowa," *Des Moines Register,* July 22, 2003.

Unsigned editorial, "The War Against Women," *New York Times,* January 12, 2003.

Vaughn, Chris, "Art, Politics and the First Lady," *Fort Worth Star-Telegram,* February 21, 2003.

Vulliamy, Ed, "The President Rides Out," *The Observer,* January 26, 2003.

Walsh, Kenneth T,. and Angie Cannon, "Laura's Moment," *U.S. News & World Report,* April 30, 2001.

Weeks, Linton, "National Chapters," *Washington Post,* September 10, 2001.

Whitehouse, Beth, "Avoiding the Spotlight," *Newsday,* January 4, 2001.

Wildman, Sarah, "Portrait of a Lady: How Laura Bush Conquered Feminism," *New Republic,* August 20, 2001.

Woodwood, Bob, *Bush at War,* New York: Simon & Schuster, 2002, 170–72.

INDEX

Abdullah, Saudi Crown Prince, 182
Acosta, Adele, 123, 124
Adams, Ashleigh, 155
Afghan Children's Fund, 168, 179
Afghan women, rights of, 178–79
Albaugh, Joe, 102
Al Qaeda, 178
Alvarez, Julia, 186
Ambrose, Stephen, 118
American Library Association, 42, 184
Anderson, Dee, 150
Anderson, Marian, 116
Applewhite, Scott, 133
Arbusto, 69
Atwater, Lee, 81
Audioslave, 156
Austin:
    Community Court in, 153
    Governor's Mansion in, 88, 90, 92, 94, 138
    inaugural events in, 92–93
    political wives in, 103
    social life in, 39–40, 41, 100, 107, 108
    state capitol in, 95
    Texas Book Festival in, 94–97
    women's book club in, 97, 100, 108
Austin American-Statesman, 95

Ball, Andrea, 101–2
Ball, David, 154–55
Barbour, Haley, 99
Beatles, 22
Beers, Charlotte, 179
Best Little Whorehouse in Texas, The (King), 95
Betts, Roland, 84
Bible, 96, 122
bin Laden, Osama, 21, 172, 178
Bird, Sarah, 93–94
bird-watching, 16
Boyd, C. Lane, 10, 55, 78–79
Bridges, William Ashe, 149–50
Brillstein-Gray, 156
Brinker, Nancy, 85

Broadmoor Hotel, Colorado Springs, 74–75
Brock, Beverly, 11
Brown v. Board of Education, 27
Buck, Steve, 12, 26–27
Burka, Paul, 61, 98, 102, 103, 105, 108, 142–43
Burns, Bobby, 11
Burns, Denise, 11
Bush, Barbara (daughter), 67, 68, 137–57
    birth and babyhood of, 70–72
    childhood of, 81, 82, 83, 84, 85
    and father's career, 92, 135–36, 137–42, 143, 144–45, 147–48, 156
    media stories about, 148, 152, 153–55, 156–57
    permissiveness toward, 135–37, 139, 140–42, 144–45, 151–52
    personal traits of, 68, 71, 136–37, 141
    public image of, 157
    and reading programs, 117
    schooling of, 85, 94, 126, 138, 141, 145
    and security detail, 135, 139, 142, 149–52
    teen years of, 90, 140–42, 150–57
    at twenty-one, 155–56
Bush, Barbara (mother-in-law), xi, 17
    and discrimination, 28
    and grandchildren, 148, 155
    and Laura, 48, 49, 50, 51–52, 58, 89, 117, 177
    and literacy issue, 93
    personal traits of, 68, 93, 110
    and political life, 57, 81–82, 83, 85, 86, 113
    in West Texas, 18
Bush, Columba, xi
Bush, Doro Koch, 117, 168
Bush, Dorothy Walker, 51–52
Bush, George H. W.:
    career of, 46, 49, 57, 62, 68, 74, 80, 83, 84, 135, 137
    desk of, 131
    and grandchildren, 155
    and Laura, 49, 65, 117
    presidential campaigns of, 80–81, 82–83, 86, 89, 132

Bush, George H. W. (cont.):
and Republican Party, 10
and son's presidency, 109, 146
in West Texas, 18, 25
Bush, George W., 45–66
achievements of, 86–87, 135
autobiography of, 48, 85
biographies of, 59, 62, 74, 82, 84
building an image, 83–84, 85, 86
and children, 68–71, 140, 141, 145–46, 151,
152, 155, 157
at Crawford ranch, 131, 178
daily routine of, 86
early years of, 28, 45–46, 63, 153, 155
and education issue, 38, 43, 104, 119–25,
127, 128, 184
engagement of Laura and, 49–51
and Enron, 10
and evangelical Christianity, 78–79, 178
and family business (politics), 58–59, 62,
80–81, 82–83, 86–87, 110, 137, 144
family concerns of, 16–17, 69, 137
as governor, 90, 93, 94–95, 98, 101, 104–5,
117, 140
in Houston, 39
inauguration of, 147–48
interests of, 16
and Laura, dating, 44, 47–49
Laura described by, 65, 76, 85, 91, 102,
117–18, 126, 168, 188
Laura's descriptions of, xii, 66
Laura's influence on, 21, 65, 66, 73, 74–77,
92, 99, 101, 102–5, 124–25, 127–28,
171–72
Laura's partnership with, 63–64, 65, 91–92,
99, 100, 101, 104–5, 126, 136, 169
marriage of, 49, 51, 53–55
media stories about, 77, 79, 82, 85, 90–92,
105, 170–71
in Midland, 10, 46–47
and money matters, 46, 72–73, 80, 84, 86
and oil business, 46, 62, 69, 72–73, 77, 80
personal traits of, 21, 45, 48, 50, 60, 63, 65,
68, 72, 74, 75–76, 91, 106, 109, 145–46,
170
political career of, 52, 57, 63, 70, 75–76,
82–84, 86–87, 89
presidency of, 92, 102, 106, 107, 109, 115,
137

presidential campaign of, 63, 64, 79, 103,
105–6, 107, 142–45
public policy of, 80, 98, 99, 129, 174,
183–84
running for Congress, 46, 48, 50, 55–57,
58–61, 62, 72, 81
running for governor, 86–87, 89
school visitations of, 119–25
and self-control, 73–74, 75–76, 78
and September 11 attacks, 160, 162,
166–67, 171, 181–82
as Shrub, 94
and Texas Rangers, 64, 84–85, 86
and Vietnam War, 45
Bush, Jeb, xi, 49, 83, 146
Bush, Jenna, 67, 68, 137–57
birth and babyhood of, 70–72
childhood of, 81, 82, 83, 84, 85
and father's career, 92, 135–36, 137–42,
143, 144–45, 147–48, 156
media stories about, 148, 149–57
permissiveness toward, 135–37, 139,
140–42, 144–45, 151–52
personal traits of, 68, 71, 136–37, 141
public image of, 157
schooling of, 85, 94, 107, 126, 138, 141, 145
and security detail, 135, 139, 142, 149–52
teen years of, 90, 140–42, 150–57
trip to Europe, 133–35, 136
at twenty-one, 155–56
Bush, Laura Welch:
activities and interests of, x–xi, xii, 16, 52,
80, 115, 132, 178
adaptability of, xi, xiii, 13, 58, 63, 66, 91,
125–26
authenticity of, 38, 64–65, 67, 76, 98
and baseball, 84–85, 87, 169
and Bush family, 51–52, 56–57, 61–63, 90
and Bush family business, xi–xii, 47, 57,
62–63, 82–83, 86–87, 110, 144
concern for her staff, 164–65, 166
at Crawford ranch, 16, 114, 126, 128–31,
178
daily routine of, 86
DAR induction of, 116
early years of, *see* Welch, Laura Lane
and education issue, 37–38, 43, 47, 94, 96,
102–4, 114, 119–25, 126–28, 157, 160,
166, 180, 184–85, 188

in Europe, 128, 133–35, 180–81, 183
exercise of, 169
fears of, 169–71
as first lady of Texas, 88–104, 174
as first lady of U.S., xii–xiii, xiv, 21, 61–62,
  68, 107–8, 109–16, 119, 124–26, 128–29,
  132, 160, 164–69, 170–73, 174–75,
  179–85, 187–88
first state dinner of, 158–59
friends of, xi, xiii, 20, 62, 74–75, 80, 89, 90,
  97, 99–101, 116, 132, 168, 174
independence of, x–xi, xii, 51, 52, 112, 114,
  174
integrity of, xi, 63, 174
lifestyle choices of, 78–80
and literacy issue, 93, 95, 96, 102, 103–4,
  185
literary salon of, 175–77
loyalty of, xi, xiii, 61, 63, 83, 188
marriage of, 49, 51, 53–55, 57
media interviews of, xii, 61, 64–65, 67, 76,
  77, 90–92, 95, 100, 112, 113–14, 116, 119,
  125, 127–28, 170–71, 182, 183
and motherhood, 67, 68–72, 82, 88, 136–37,
  138–42, 146, 148, 151, 152, 156, 157
move to Austin, 92
move to Dallas, 83, 84–85, 87
move to Washington, 81–82, 132
myths about, ix–x, 13
personal traits of, xi–xii, 54, 57–58, 61–66,
  68, 76, 97–99, 102, 107, 109, 113, 127–28,
  163, 171, 188
and policy advisers, 102
and political campaigns, 55–56, 59–61, 62,
  64, 82–83, 89, 105–6, 109, 142–45
and pregnancy, 68–70, 137
privacy sought by, xi–xii, 50, 68, 76, 78, 88,
  89, 90, 97, 101, 127, 170
public attitudes toward, xii, xiii, 38, 52,
  94–95, 96–97, 128
public life of, xiii–xiv, 62–63, 68, 82, 83,
  84–86, 87, 88–98, 102–8, 110
public speeches by, xiii, 56, 90–91, 93–94,
  99, 103, 109, 123, 126, 163, 168, 179–80
as reader, xii, 38, 40–41, 43, 62, 100,
  118–19, 174, 175–78
reading programs sponsored by, 92–97,
  106–7, 115–19, 159, 174–75, 185–87
relaxation techniques of, ix–x, 19

and religion, 78–79
school visitations of, 119–25
and security detail, 97, 101, 129, 132, 162
as self-sustaining, 166, 169
and September 11 attacks, 159–66, 171,
  172–73
signature style of, 97, 125–26, 129
as supportive of husband, xi, xii, xiii, 31,
  53, 55–56, 61, 63, 66, 74–76, 81, 87,
  89–92, 112, 125, 127, 128, 168–71,
  181–82, 187–88
as teacher, xii, 37, 95
and White House, 132
Bush, Marvin, 57, 168
Bush, Neil, 75
Bush at War (Woodward), 170
Bush family:
  being true to oneself in, 63
  loyalty in, 81, 83
  media criticism of, 86
  politics as business of, xi–xii, 47, 57,
    58–59, 62–63, 80–81, 82–83, 86–87, 110,
    137, 144
  time together with, 168–69
Byrd, Lee, 101

Cafritz, Peggy Cooper, 125
Caldwell, Sarah, 52
Card, Andy, 164
Card, Rev. Kathleene, 164, 166
Carlos, John, 27
Carpenter, Liz, 92
Carter, Rosalynn, 52
Cather, Willa, 176
Central Intelligence Agency (CIA), 49
César Chávez Elementary School,
  Hyattsville, 124
Charge to Keep, A (Bush), 85
Charlotte's Web (White), 36
Chase, Bob, 124
Cheers Shot Bar, Austin, 153, 156
Cheney, Dick, 64, 107, 117
Cheney, Lynne, 117, 126
Chiles, Eddie, 84
Chirac, Jacques, 63
Cisneros, Sandra, 96
civil rights movement, 26, 33
Clark, Carol Higgins, 118
Clark, Mary Higgins, 118

Clark, Torie, 179

Clements, Bill, 103

Clements, Rita, 103

Clifford the Big Red Dog, 159

Clinton, Bill, 83, 86, 147, 150

Clinton, Chelsea, 142, 144, 148–49, 152

Clinton, Hillary Rodham, 113, 117, 147
   as proactive first lady, xiv, 91–92, 102, 110,
     111, 126
   on role of first lady, 188
   and September 11 attacks, 162

Coleman, Viola, 28–29

Collins, Billy, 186, 187

Collins, Gail, 153

Combs, Sean "Puffy," 156

Connally, John, 103

Connally, Nellie, 103

Copper Canyon Press, 186

Cornell, Chris, 156

Country Music Awards, 116

Couric, Katie, 112

Craig, Dottie, 18–19, 28

Craig, Earle, 18, 28

Crawford, Texas, ranch, 16, 114, 126, 128–31,
   178, 188

Crouch, Stanley, 118

C-SPAN, 175

Curtis, Charlotte, 52

Curtis, Tracy and Greg, 108

Dallas Morning News, 90–92

DAR Constitution Hall, Washington,
   115–16

Dawson, Mollie, 53

Dawson Elementary School, Austin, 41–43,
   47, 94, 95, 120

Dewhurst, David, 11–12

Dewitt, Bill, 84

Dickinson, Emily, 185, 187

Domingo, Placido, 159

Douglas, Michael, 3–9, 25, 67, 137

Du Bois, W. E. B., 176

Dykes, Judy, 3

Earle, Elisabeth, 153

Earth Liberation Front, 129

Eastwood, Clint, 159

Eisenhower, Mamie, xiv, 57

Enron Corporation, 10

Episcopal Seminary of the Southwest, 99

Equal Rights Amendment (ERA), 60

Evans, Don, 62, 73, 74–75

Evans, Susie, 62, 73, 74–75

Farabee, Mary Margaret, 96–97, 98, 99–100,
   132

Fehrenbach, T. R., 94

Feminine Mystique, The (Friedan), 35

Ferber, Edna, 176–77

Fern, Charlene, 98, 103, 164

first lady, roles of, xiv, 110–14, 125, 174–75,
   179–85, 188

First Son (Minutaglio), 59, 74, 82, 84

First United Methodist Church, Midland,
   54–55, 78–79

Fleischer, Ari, 155

Flight 93, Pennsylvania, 166

FLOTUS (First Lady of the United States),
   133

Flowers, Gennifer, 86

Fontenot, Jane Ann, 20, 23, 24, 80, 99

Fox, Vicente, 158

Friedan, Betty, 35

Friedman, Kinky, 99

Gammon, Billy, 41, 43–44, 48

Gammon, Regan:
   and book group, 97, 100
   on George and Laura, 48, 50
   as Jenna's godmother, 145
   as Laura's friend, 20, 41, 64, 80, 89, 99, 129,
     132
   and Midland memories, 4–5, 22

Gass, William H., 177

Gates of the Alamo, The (Harrigan), 93, 118

Gatson, Larry, 38

Georgetown University, early childhood
   education summit, 126–28

Giant (Ferber), 176

Gnagy, Charlene, 32, 117

Gore, Al, 64, 105, 107, 147

Gore, Tipper, 64, 147

Graham, Rev. Billy, 78

Graham, Katharine, 52

Gramm, Phil, 101

Gregg, Judd, 162

Gregorian, Vartan, 177

Gregory, David, 63, 105

Gunesch, Tobia Hochman, 5, 21, 22, 33
Gunnells, Vestophia, 38

Hamill, Sam, 186, 187
Hance, Kent, 58–60
Harden, Alison, 161
Harken Energy Corp., 80, 84
Harlem Renaissance, 175
Harrigan, Stephen, 93, 95, 97, 100, 107, 118
Hart, Gary, 74
Havel, Václav, 181
Hawkins, Harold, 15
Hawkins, Jessie, 14–15
HBO specials, 116
Head Start, 94, 104, 127
Hepburn, Audrey, 57
Heymann, David, 129–31
Hidden Power (Marton), 112–13
Highland Park United Methodist Church,
    Dallas, 85
Hitler, Adolf, 181
Hockaday School, Dallas, 85
Holden, Bob, 123
Houston, Sam, 88
Houston, Whitney, 116
Huegel, Christina, 97–98
Hughes, Karen, 48, 101, 165, 171, 179, 180
Hughes, Langston, 175, 176, 185, 187
Hunt, Al, 73–74
Hurston, Zora Neale, 175

"I Love You, Little One" (children's reader),
    167
"In Defense of the Book" (Gass), 177
Indianapolis Junior League, 155
Ivins, Molly, 94

Jeffords, Jim, 162
Jeopardy! (TV), 116
Johnson, Ann, 62
Johnson, Clay, 62
Johnson, Lady Bird, 52, 82, 92, 95, 113–14
Johnson, Lyndon Baines, 27, 33, 37, 92
Journeys with George (Pelosi), 79

Kelton, Elmer, 94
Kemp, Jack, 74
Kendrick, Phil, 80
Kennedy, Edward M., 37, 127, 160, 161–63, 184

Kennedy, Jacqueline Bouvier, 132
Kennedy, John F., 5, 27–28, 162, 169
Kent State University, 33
Kincaid, Jamaica, 186
King, Billie Jean, 52
King, Larry, 115, 128
King, Larry L., 95, 96
King, Martin Luther, Jr., 33
Kinnell, Galway, 187
Kipen, David, 118
Kiss, The, 64–65
Komen Foundation, 85
Ku Klux Klan, 25
Kutcher, Ashton, 156

Laney, Pete, 102
Lawrence, Mary Wells, 53
Lawrence, Mia, 154
Lee, Dixie Ray, 52
Lee, Robert E., 7
Lewis, David Levering, 175–76
Limerick, Patricia Nelson, 176–77
Locked in the Cabinet (Reich), 97
Longley, Joe, 39–40
Longley, Susan, 39
Lugar, Richard, 74
Lyon, Billy, 122

McAninch, Jim, 73
McCarroll, Jimmy, 39–40
McCarthy, Eugene, 11
McClellan, Scott, 155
McClesky, Robert:
    on Bush children, 151
    on George and Laura as team, 65
    and Midland memories, 4, 15, 19, 23, 46
McCrane-Kashmere Gardens Library,
    Houston, 41
McKinnon, Mark, 105, 106
McLeese, Don, 95
McMurtry, Larry, 94
McQuillan, Larry, 163
Malcolm, Andrew, 49
Manley, Jim, 161
Margo, Adair, 100, 101
Marton, Kati, 112–13
Matalin, Mary, 179
Mayflower, 51, 116
Mesnier, Roland, 158

Michener, James, 94
Midland, Texas:
  auto accident in, 1–9, 30–31, 67, 76, 119,
    137, 170
  Bush wedding in, 54–55
  discrimination in, 12, 25–27, 28–30, 176
  as dry town, 22
  economic slump in, 73, 77
  family life in, 71–72
  First United Methodist Church in, 54–55,
    78–79
  geography of, *see* West Texas
  Greentree Country Club in, 12
  high schools in, 3, 6–8, 22–30
  Petroleum Club in, 9, 10, 24
  Republican Women in, 9, 10–12
  social change in, 12, 27, 29
  social life in, 9–10, 12, 17, 19–20, 23–27, 29,
    62, 73
  teen years in, 21–30
  transplants to, 18–20
Minutaglio, Bill, 59, 62, 74, 82, 84
Moline Elementary School, St. Louis, 122–23,
  151
Munn, Bill, 62
Munn, Lynn, 58, 62, 100
  and Bush moves, 81, 83
  and Midland memories, 19, 73
  on motherhood, 69, 70–71, 146–47
Murphy, Eddie, 116

National Book Festival, 159
National Education Association (NEA), 124,
  184
National Enquirer, 150
National Press Club, 168, 186
Nelson, Pam, 39
Nelson, Ricky, 21
Nelson, Willie, 39–40
New Republic, 112, 125, 127
Newsweek, 170
New York Times, 153
Nixon, Pat, 92
"No child left behind," 103–4, 119–20, 124,
  184
Nowlin, Susan, 34

O'Neill, Jan Donnelly, 34, 72
  friendship of, 20, 62, 74–75

with George and Laura, 46, 47, 49–50
O'Neill, Joe, 46, 47, 49, 62, 74–75
Organisation for Economic Co-operation
    and Development (OECD), 180
Osama bin Laden, 21, 172, 178
Oswald, Lee Harvey, 27

Paige, Rod, 124, 126, 184
Patriot Act, 184
Paul Quinn College, Dallas, 85
Pelosi, Alexandra, 79
Pelosi, Nancy, 79
Pentagon, September 11 attack on, 163–64
Petroleum Club, Midland, 9, 10, 24
Petty, Marge, 20, 80
"Poetry and the American Voice," 185–87
Porter, Katherine Anne, 176
Posen, Zac, 156
Powell, James, 132

Radio Free Europe, 179
Rampersad, Arnold, 176
"Ready to Read" initiative, 104
Reagan, Nancy, 95, 110
Reagan, Ronald, 62, 112, 170
Rebelee yearbook (1964), 6–8, 20, 21
Rehnquist, William, 147
Reich, Robert, 97
Republican National Convention:
  (1988), 82
  (1996), 99, 109
  (2000), 76, 109
Rice, Condoleezza, 48, 107
Richards, Ann, 89, 103, 138
Riss, Sarah, 123
Robert E. Lee High School, Midland, 3, 6–8,
  24, 26, 30
Rodriguez, Noelia, 102, 115, 124–25, 127–28,
  170
Rogers, Clifford, 154
Rolling Stone, 156
Roosevelt, Eleanor, 173
Roosevelt, Franklin D., 112
Rose, Edward "Rusty," 84
Rose, Lela, 147
Rove, Karl, xi, 60, 119
Royall, Penny, 75
Rumpus (Yale magazine), 150–51
Russell, Doug, 27

Russert, Tim, 145
Ryan, Nolan, 84
Ryerson, Mary Ann, 19, 22, 23, 26, 29, 33

Sadler, Paul, 103
Safady, Eddie, 98–99
Sain, Ken, 97
St. Andrew's Episcopal School, Austin, 94,
    138, 141
Saudi Arabia, women in, 182–83
Schroeder, Patricia, 111
Sciolino, Elaine, 117
September 11 attacks, 159–73, 181–82
Shaffer, Debbie, 42
Shrake, Bud, 39
Smith, Terral, 101, 104, 105, 141
Smith, Tommie, 27
Sobieraj, Sandra, 183
Southern Methodist University, 32–35, 48
Spellings, Margaret LaMontagne, 104, 125
Spitz, Mark, 27
Splash (dog), 162
Stewart, Anne Lund, 51
Stewart, Shannon, 154
Stowe, Harriet Beecher, 118
Student Nonviolent Coordinating
    Committee (SNCC), 26
Sullivant Elementary School, Columbus,
    120–21
Supreme Court, U.S., 106, 107
Susan G. Komen Breast Cancer Foundation,
    85

Taft, Bob, 142
Taliban, 166, 178, 179, 181
Teach for America, 124, 157
Terry, Marshall, 33
Texas, zero tolerance in, 154
Texas Air National Guard, 45, 46
Texas Alcoholic Beverage Commission,
    154–55
Texas authors, 93–94, 96
Texas Book Festival, 94–97, 106–7, 115, 132
Texas Department of Public Safety, troopers
    from, 97, 101, 139
Texas Rangers, 64, 84–85, 86
Theresienstadt, visit to, xiii, 181
Thompson, Tommy, 126
Tower, John, 85

Troops to Teachers, 124, 128
Twain, Mark, 175

Uncle Tom's Cabin (Stowe), 118
United Nations (UN), 60
United Nations Population Fund, 183
United Way, 70
University of Texas, 25, 26, 38–39, 93, 94, 107,
    145, 154
Upshaw, Dawn, 159
U.S. News & World Report, 152

Vietnam War, 33, 45
Voting Rights Act, 37

Walker, Jerry Jeff, 40
Walker, Mary Willis, 94
Walter Reed Army Medical Center,
    Washington, 165
Walters, Barbara, 52
Washingtonian, 74
Washington Post, 110, 171
Wead, Doug, 143–44
Weaver, Reg, 184
Weiss, Nancy, 76
Weiss, Peggy Porter, 20, 22, 80, 132
Welch, Harold:
    aging of, 90
    childhood of, 13
    death of, 9
    and grandchildren, 71
    and Laura's early years, 1, 3, 17, 35
    and Laura's wedding, 53
    marriage of Jenna and, 15, 18
    personal traits of, 15
    socializing, 9
Welch, Jenna Hawkins:
    activities and interests of, 15–16
    DAR induction of, 116
    family background of, 13, 14–15
    and George, 48
    and grandchildren, 68, 71
    health of, 90
    and Laura's early years, 1, 3, 16–17, 20, 32,
        35, 38, 103
    and Laura's wedding, 54
    marriage of Harold and, 15, 18
    in Midland, 10–11, 12, 21, 107
    and reading programs, 117

Welch, Laura Lane:
  in auto accident, 1–9, 30–31, 67, 76, 119, 137, 170
  birth and background of, 13–27, 56, 103
  college years of, 32–35
  as debutante, 34
  and Democrats, 11
  engagement of George and, 49–51
  in Europe, 35–36
  and George, dating, 44, 47–49
  high-school yearbook of, 6–8, 20, 21
  as librarian, 30, 39, 41–43, 44, 53, 99, 118, 120
  marriage of, *see* Bush, Laura Welch
  personal traits of, 30–31, 48, 50
  social life of, 39–41, 44, 47, 48
  as teacher, 27, 32, 35, 36–38, 104, 117
Welch, Lula Lane, 13
Welch, Mark, 13, 35
West Texas:
  campaigning in, 56–61, 62
  droughts in, 18–19
  oil business in, 9, 18, 20, 22, 24–25, 31, 46, 62, 72–73, 77
  political parties in, 10–11, 27
  roots in, xiv, 13–20, 31, 51, 95
  survival in, 14, 19
  women's roles in, 12–13, 14, 17–18, 20–21, 31
  see also Midland, Texas
Whatever the Wind Delivers, 13–14
White, E. B., 36

Whitman, Walt, 185, 187
Wilder, Laura Ingalls, 176
Wildman, Sarah, 112, 125, 127
Williams, Tony, 128
Wilson, Eddie, 40
Wilson, Edith, 173
Wilson, Woodrow, 112
Wolfman, Cathryn, 45, 48, 49
women, roles of:
  in adapting to husband's interests, 57, 68
  authors, 176–77
  and basic rights, 178–79, 182–83, 188
  and feminism, 112, 125
  and health issues, 183
  political, 52, 103, 112–13, 179–84
  and power, 52–53, 112–13, 114, 115, 125
  and strength, 169
  traditional, 123
  in West Texas, 12–13, 14, 17–18, 20–21, 31
Woodruff, Judy, 73–74
Woodward, Bob, 170, 171
World Trade Center, New York, 161
World War I, 173
World War II, 173, 181
Wright, Lawrence, 94

Yale University, 145
Young, Andrew, 60
Younger, Charles, 50

Zambelli fireworks, 159
Zelis, Vickie, 42, 43, 44, 51

ABOUT THE AUTHOR

Ann Gerhart has been a writer at the *Style* section of *The Washington Post* since 1995, and wrote the paper's Reliable Source column for three and a half years. She lives in Bethesda, Maryland, with her husband and three children.